New Ways of Writing
A Handbook for Writing with Computers

New Ways of Writing
A Handbook for Writing with Computers

Susan Miller
University of Utah

Kyle Knowles
University of Utah

A Blair Press Book

PRENTICE HALL, Upper Saddle River, New Jersey 07458

Library of Congress Cataloging–in–Publication Data
Miller, Susan
    New ways of writing : a handbook for writing with computers /
Susan Miller and Kyle Knowles.
        p.   cm.
    Includes bibliographical references and index.
    ISBN 0–13–531260–4
    1. English language—Rhetoric—Data processing—Handbooks,
manuals, etc.   2. Word processing in education—Handbooks, manuals,
etc.   3. Academic writing—Handbooks, manuals, etc.   I. Knowles,
Kyle.   II. Title.
PE1408.M5537   1997
808'.042'0285—dc20   96–23868
                                                          CIP

Editorial Director: Charlyce Jones Owen
Publisher: Nancy Perry
Executive Editor: Mary Jo Southern
Director of Production and Manufacturing: Barbara Kittle
Managing Editor: Bonnie Biller
Editorial/Production Supervision: Mary Rottino
Manufacturing Manager: Nick Sklitsis
Prepress and Manufacturing Buyer: Robert Anderson
Creative Design Director: Leslie Osher
Art Director: Carole Anson
Interior and Cover Design: Siren Design, Inc.

Figure credits and trademark information may be found on page 189,
which should be considered an extension of the copyright page.

This book was set in Modern MT Extended by Pine Tree Composition
and was printed by Courier (Westford, MA). The cover was printed by Phoenix
Color Corporation.

A Blair Press Book

© 1997 by Prentice-Hall, Inc.
Simon & Schuster/A Viacom Company
Upper Saddle River, New Jersey 07458

Printed in the United States of America
10 9 8 7 6 5 4 3 2 1

ISBN 0-13-531260-4 (spiral)
ISBN 0-13-652215-7 (paper)

Prentice-Hall International (UK) Limited, *London*
Prentice-Hall of Australia Pty. Limited, *Sydney*
Prentice-Hall Canada, Inc., *Toronto*
Prentice-Hall Hispanoamerica, S.A., *Mexico*
Prentice-Hall of India Private Limited, *New Delhi*
Prentice-Hall of Japan, Inc., *Tokyo*
Simon & Schuster Asia Pte. Ltd., *Singapore*
Editoria Prentice-Hall do Brasil, Ltda., *Rio de Janiero*

→ PREFACE ←

We wrote this book about writing with computers because our work with students, teachers, and people who administer computer systems tells us that most of the information available about this new technology misses the specific needs of people who write. People who write with a computer do not care so much about what it can do as they care about what they can do with it—as easily as possible. They want to make their writing and editing more effective and efficient, communicate through e-mail, and find and use the information that is available from electronic sources. We answer questions every day from people who need to take advantage of these and the many other new ways of writing that computers have made available but who find little help that is directly to the point.

New Ways of Writing is a guide through both generalized and specific writing processes and ways of producing texts. Its four parts move from the individual writer who is using a computer to create a document to exchanges of data and ideas among many networked computers and writers. This movement from isolated to connected uses of computers is presented, cross-referenced, and indexed in handbook form. You can skip or quickly review basics you already know and turn to unfamiliar information when you need specific help.

The first part of the book, "One Writer, One Computer," covers the basics of using a computer to write. It takes you through both extended and abbreviated processes for writing a document. It describes editing with a computer and tells how to format and print a document. Part Two, "One Writer, Many Kinds of Writing," explains how a computer can help you write specific kinds of academic, personal, and professional documents, including ongoing journals and notes, essays, researched documents, reports, letters and memos, résumés, exams, and creative writing. This second part also describes options for publishing your writing, both personally and professionally, with word processing or desktop publishing programs.

Part Three, "One Writer, Many Computers," explains uses of Internet resources. It answers common questions about connecting to electronic forms of information as you research and write your own documents. Part Four, "Many Writers, Many Computers," focuses on conversations that occur only with connected computers. It describes conventional ways of writing e-mail and using news groups and discussion lists, tells how to form groups that use e-mail to discuss writing and reading, and provides information about real-time (synchronous) electronic conversations. This part closes with a chapter that describes using the World Wide Web to find and circulate information, view media, make purchases, and communicate directly with others.

Computer technologies and the Internet expand much traditional wisdom about writing. They encourage writers to think, revise, and edit simultaneously. They make it easier to share writing-in-progress with others who can contribute to it before it is finished, and to publish finished documents for a great number of individuals and groups. They allow anyone who writes to contribute to and participate in many entertaining, informative, and powerful group discussions. But all of these fresh possibilities for written communication require specific new knowledge about how to use computers and the Internet actively.

New ways of writing should not, we think, lead writers to forget the importance of attention to effective composing. The topics we discuss combine how-to's of technology with information about thoughtful planning, thorough revising, and careful editing, to help you create efficient and accurate language that best fits specific situations and readers. We focus on helpful suggestions that can make computers not only tools for writing but participants in your success in a range of writing situations.

The general principle that has guided our selection and organization of materials is that writing with computers is best learned in steps. There is no right way to become a skillful computer user, nor do experienced users share precisely the same techniques and knowledge. As you become more practiced in using a computer and undertake new purposes in writing for various readers, you will find yourself forming an expanding and changing set of habits that fits the technology you have available and the time you have to learn how to use it. We hope this ready reference will help you practice with computers in many writing situations, to create your own new ways of writing.

Acknowledgments

We want to thank many people who helped make this book possible. We have had excellent advice and editorial support from Nancy Perry and Mary Jo Southern at Prentice Hall and from Dona Hickey (University of Richmond) and John Hollowell (University of California, Irvine). The faculty members and graduate students in the University Writing Program and the staff of the Marriott Library Multimedia Center have been generous with their time and suggestions, as have John Halleck, Computer Center, and Professor Lee Hollaar, Computer Science, at the University of Utah.

We are very grateful to the following colleagues who took time to review *New Ways of Writing* in its earliest version: F. G. Bench, University of Wisconsin, Platteville; Michael Clark, Widener University; Eric Crump, University of Missouri, Columbia; Ron Fortune, Illinois State University; Sarah Haimowitz; Marcia Peoples Halio, University of Delaware; Muriel Harris, Purdue University; Deborah H. Holdstein, Governors State University; Beth Kolko, University of Wyoming.

We also want to thank the teachers who tested this book in their classes as well as their students for very helpful comments that guided many revisions. We thank Janice Neuleib, Illinois State University; Michael Petracca, University of California at Santa Barbara; Gregory Rode, University of Utah; Jacqueline Stahl Skibine, University of Utah.

Finally, our decisions about what to include in *New Ways of Writing* were often guided by responses to a lengthy questionnaire. The following people gave us a realistic picture of the computer experience and habits of a broad range of readers. We thank Craig Bartholomaus, University of Missouri, Kansas City; Chris Brock, North Harris College; Ted Brown, Murray State University; Cheryl M. Cassidy, Eastern Michigan University; Irene L. Clark, University of Southern California; Dan Davis Jr., University of Houston; Kitty Dean, Nassau Community College; Robert Dial, University of Akron; Christine Farris, Indiana University; Samuel J. Goldstein, Daytona Beach Community College; Barbara Gross, Rutgers University; Donna Hatford, Texas A&M University at Kingsville; Jennifer Jordan-Henly, Roane State Community College; Kathleen M. Hermdom, Weber State University; Eleanor James, Montgomery Community College; Julie King, University of Wisconsin—Parkside; Melinda Kramer, Prince George's Community College; Kay M. Losey, University of North Carolina, Chapel Hill; Barry M. Maid, University of Arkansas at Little Rock; Janet Matthews, Milwaukee Area Technical College; Linda B. Moore, University of Western Florida; David C. Owens, Friends University; Irvin Peckham, University of Omaha; J. Persoon, Grand Valley State University; Stephen Reid, Colorado State University; Janine Rider, Mesa State College; David Roberts, Samford University; Kate Ronald, University of Nebraska; Carol Scheidenhelm, Northern Illinois University; Linda A. Schuller, Bowling Green State University; Helen J. Schwartz, Indiana University—Purdue University Indianapolis; Robert T. Self, Northern Illinois University; Jack Selzer, Pennsylvania State University; Elizabeth Sommers, San Francisco State University; Chris Thaiss, George Mason University; Nancy M. Walczyk, University of Wisconsin—Milwaukee; Mike Williams, New Mexico Junior College.

Susan Miller
Kyle Knowles
http://www.prenhall.com/miller

How to Read this Book with Its Web Site

New Ways of Writing has its own welcome page on the World Wide Web, at the address http://www.prenhall.com/miller. This page contains a table of contents, with links to chapter overviews. This page also has links to all the Internet addresses we mention in the book. From the Web page you can connect to library resources and electronic documents. We encourage your comments and will use them to update *New Ways of Writing*.

CONTENTS

Chapter 6   Printing Your Documents   50

PART TWO
One Writer, Many Kinds of Writing

Chapter 7   Ongoing Compositions: Records and Notes   56

Chapter 8   Essays and Other Assigned Writing   62

Chapter 11   Letters and Memos   93

Chapter 12   Résumés   101

Chapter 13   Taking Examinations   107

New Ways of Writing
A Handbook for Writing
with Computers

PART ONE

One Writer, One Computer

1
Writing with a Computer

1a Why Write with a Computer?

    1a–1 Computers are active memory systems.

    1a–2 Computers show alternative versions of your writing.

    1a–3 Computers help you edit.

    1a–4 Word processing allows you to express voice, tone, and special emphases visually.

1b Experimenting with New Ways of Writing

1c Working within the Limitations of Word Processing

    1c–1 "My computer can't do that."

    1c–2 "My word processor doesn't do that."

    1c–3 "Do you have some paper?"

    1c–4 "It looks so good, it must be good."

    1c–5 "However, I spill checked."

1d New Time-Saving Habits

    1d–1 Habits that save time as you start writing

    1d–2 Habits that save time as you write

    1d–3 Habits that save time as you finish writing

The Next Time You Write

1a

This chapter describes the many ways that computers help writers become faster and more skillful. It reviews the possibilities that word processing offers, notes some limitations of writing with computers, and suggests ways to address those limitations. It also lists ways that word processing saves time as you prepare, write, and complete projects.

1a Why Write with a Computer?

Many writers apply the same methods whenever they write, no matter what tools they use, and have fine results. But a computer is an especially valuable writing tool because its technological functions encourage you to vary, combine, and rethink your writing processes to fit your goals and the time allotted for a specific writing situation. A computer makes it easier to think and write simultaneously, helps you become a better editor, and improves the appearance of your finished writing. The following unique features of computers can help you in specific writing situations.

1a-1 Computers are active memory systems.

Word processing software is designed much like a filing cabinet. It allows you to organize, store, and find notes and passages you have written any time you want them. It can retrieve an entire file for a piece of writing from the computer's electronic storage system and transfer all or parts of it to new work. It eliminates unnecessary retyping.

When you open a saved file, you can improve and rework it. If you open two or more saved files at once, you can combine them or move between them as you write.

You can view lists of all the names of your saved files, which are located in the computer's folders or directories. You can view file names in alphabetical order, in the order of the last date you closed them, or in other sequences. If the list shows the time you last changed a document, you can refer to it to see your progress on any file.

You can take a file you create in one word processing program and save it in another word processing format for use by other writers at their own computers. For instance, using the Save As command, you can save a WordPerfect® document as a Microsoft Word® document or as "text only."

1a-2 Computers show alternative versions of your writing.

With word processing you can see your writing from a variety of perspectives, you can vary how you see your writing as you draft and edit, and you can choose how printed pages will look. For example, you can make the

Figure 1.1   Two Document Files Opened Simultaneously

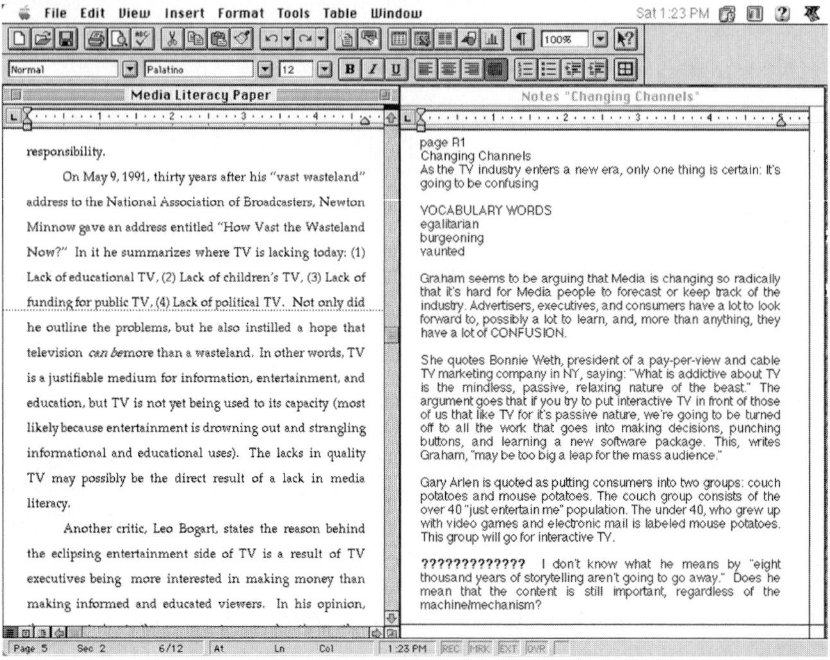

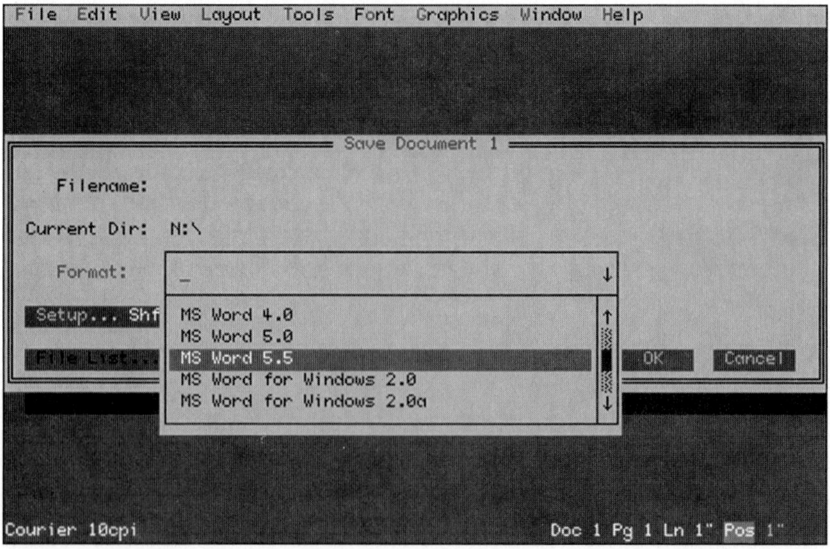

Figure 1.2   "Save As" from WordPerfect to Microsoft Word

space for writing larger or smaller; you can scroll through a document continuously or screen by screen; or you can jump to the top or bottom of a paragraph or go back to earlier insertion points.

You can experiment with indentations, line spacing, margins, and the text that will appear at the top or bottom of each page. You can use word processing to make or insert columns of text, tables, graphs, charts, and drawings.

1a–3 Computers help you edit.

Writing with a word processing program gives you more time to focus on decisions about content and effective style because it allows you to make quick changes while you write and helps you revise and correct later. You can quickly move to a place where you notice a change is needed. You can copy and move words or passages or delete them, either temporarily or permanently.

You can also search through documents for words and phrases that you want to change. You can check the spelling of words, change obvious misspellings, and find alternative choices for words in a built-in spell checker, grammar checker, and thesaurus.

1a–4 Word processing allows you to express voice, tone, and special emphases visually.

You can show letters and symbols in different styles and sizes and in various forms of visual emphases (capitalization, underlining, and so on). Each of these possibilities helps unify your writing processes. Writing with a computer allows you simultaneously to think about what you want to say and to inflect it visually with emphases that help control how it will be read by others. This technology helps you craft language that will make your intentions vivid to readers of your finished documents.

1b Experimenting with New Ways of Writing

To take advantage of the features of word processing, keep in mind the following guidelines.

1. Familiarize yourself with the basic features of your word processing program. Most word processing software has the same basic features.

2. Note unfamiliar word processing features you read about, notice on your screen and in menus, or hear about from others who write with computers.

3. Look for "tools" or "commands" in menus and in your word processing manual. Activate these on-screen items to become aware of their

Figure 1.3   Writing Tools in WordPerfect

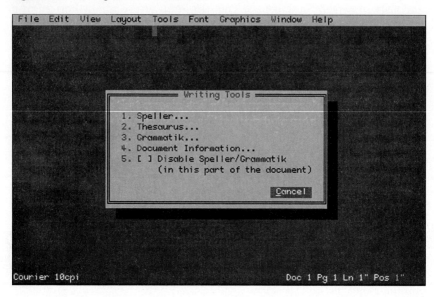

functions. Practice using new commands after you understand their effects.

4.   Remember that it is not easy to break a computer by using it. You can, of course, mistreat a computer or diskettes by dropping them, spilling something on them, or leaving them in extreme temperatures. When such accidents happen, consult a manual, ask for help from a more experienced user, or call the help line of your computer company. Usually, such mishaps are not fatal to your computer or your documents.

5.   We cannot say often enough that you should save your writing frequently. If your computer has an automatic Always Make Backups function or its equivalent, turn it on. Despite warnings, many people avoid saving frequently until they lose an important document. Learn and practice using Undo and Restore commands. They will reverse the last action you took and restore your document to its previous form if you make a mistake.

1c Working within the Limitations of Word Processing

Using word processing certainly makes writing easier, encourages improvements, and saves time. But you need to be aware of some limitations on writing with computers.

1c–1 "My computer can't do that."

Newer computers have enough memory to accomplish almost any combination of writing tasks. But many older computers still in use will not be able to accomplish everything you may want to do. For instance, you may not be able to open a word processing file while you are using your e-mail program. Sometimes limited memory also makes it impossible to save a long document on the computer you write it on, and you will need to store it on a diskette.

Depending on the operating system your computer uses, you may also need to use file names that are a specified length and use only designated punctuation marks (see 2a–1). Newer versions of some systems allow for longer file names.

1c–2 "My word processor doesn't do that."

One or more features that we discuss in this book may not be available on the word processing software you use. But it will take you some time to familiarize yourself with all the features it does have. Every so often, declare a "technology hour" to experiment with features you have never used. Unfamiliar commands may activate functions that you will want to make habitual.

Word processing programs best manage words. Specialized software more easily accomplishes some other tasks, such as making graphics and displaying data in spreadsheets. When you need it, specialized software will save time and help ensure good results. Some programs may be purchased; some are included with new computers. Some may be copied for free; others may be copied for a fee.

1c–3 "Do you have some paper?"

Obviously, it is not always suitable to write with a computer. Some writing is most conveniently composed by hand: sudden inspirations and brief notes of conversations, references and notes to information you find in odd settings, and points made in discussions or meetings where a computer is not available. Brainstorming to get ideas and arrange relationships among them may be difficult with computers because their screens are small and their words appear in lines, not in scattered arrangements. You may want to sketch your earliest plans with paper and pen, just to get started in a familiar way. But you can transfer the gist of notes and outlines to a computer file for later use.

1c–4 "It looks so good, it must be good."

Word processing enhances the appearance of every element of a piece of writing—titles, headers, section headings, text. But spending too much time on appearance may reduce the quality of the writing itself. Readers look for ideas and their development in well-reasoned points, examples, and other evidence, not in fancy visual effects.

Draft and edit before you consider the appearance of your writing. Consider how printed pages will look only after you are satisfied with content.

1c–5 "However, I spill checked."

Most word processing software is equipped with helpful spell checkers and grammar checkers, but these tools can lead you astray. A spell checker will not stop for words in its dictionary, so it will not catch errors like mistyping "bar" for "bare" or substituting "too" for "to." (Some advanced spellers will stop for words that sound like others.) Spell checkers may also offer inaccurate suggestions, for example by suggesting *alternate* where *alternative* is correct. Don't rely too heavily on spell checkers. You still must read a printed copy to catch errors.

A grammar checker may make inaccurate or unsuitable suggestions. The best use of a grammar checker is to highlight each sentence of a document for rereading.

1d New Time-Saving Habits

To get the full benefit of writing with a computer, try time-saving habits that experienced writers use as they write. As with all uses of computers and all writing, you will learn in steps by experimenting on your own and by getting help from people with experience.

You can look for time-savers as soon as you start using word processing. But do not worry too much about wasting time. You can spend so much time learning ways to save time that you have less time to write well. Practice your most useful time-saving habits until they become automatic, so you have more opportunities to think about what you want to say and improve your writing.

1d–1 Habits that save time as you start writing

● When you first start a new word processing file, name and save the file so you can close it quickly at any time without accidentally losing it.

● Transfer ideas and notes from other files to the document you are writing. Keep unused notes, ideas, and long passages you cut on a separate page at the bottom of a draft for possible future uses.

1d–2 Habits that save time as you write

● Select, copy, and paste passages instead of retyping them.

● Learn to use keystrokes for frequently used commands like Open, Save, Go back, and Find. Keystrokes execute functions more quickly than clicking on choices in menus.

TIME-SAVING HABITS

1. Always begin by naming and saving your file.
2. Keep your unused notes at the bottom of the document.
3. Never retype. Use Select, Copy, and Paste.
4. Learn and use keystrokes for frequently used commands.
5. Before closing a document, note how you want to begin your next session.
6. Postpone final formatting until you finish writing and editing.
7. Use commands that quickly reorder or renumber lists.
8. Make and use templates for the kinds of writing you do frequently.

● Draft in a font style and size you find easy to read on the screen.

● Learn and use commands that save time searching through a document to make changes. Use the Find, Go to, and Replace (sometimes Change) commands to correct repeated errors, to insert alternative words, and to develop and cut passages.

● Before ending a drafting session, note at the bottom of the document how you want to begin your next session.

1d–3 Habits that save time as you finish writing

● Postpone formatting until you finish writing and editing and are ready to print.

● Use Renumber or similar commands to rearrange numerical or alphabetical lists quickly.

● Make and use "templates," or model documents, to save time formatting documents you write frequently.

The Next Time You Write

1. Check out the meanings of unfamiliar terms in your word processing manual and on-screen menus. Practice using the functions they describe on a new document.

2. Look for functions and commands described in this chapter that are available in your word processing program. Are any unavailable? Programs uniquely name functions and commands—for instance, Quit may be equivalent to Exit in some programs—so be sure you persist before you decide you cannot find a feature you want to try.

2

Using a Computer in Extended Writing Processes

This chapter describes using a computer for an extended writing process. It tells how to combine thinking, gathering materials, drafting, and revising with the help of a computer. With word processing you can develop ideas about a topic, take notes from various sources, and explore ideas from multiple perspectives at every stage of the writing process.

Word processing can help you plan carefully and make multiple changes in a draft. The functions described here as a sequence can actually help at almost any stage during your writing.

2a Getting Started

With word processing you can record and move words so easily that it is useful at any stage: you can use it to focus on a purpose, to take notes, and to develop your ideas. You can expand on your initial notes, tag them with special characters to indicate that they need more work, erase them when they are no longer useful, move them from one place to another in the draft, and insert new ideas anywhere in the document as you draft it.

2a–1 Name a file.

Start by opening and naming a computer file for your notes. Using word processing, you must name every file (also called a document).

NAMES.   Use a consistent code or abbreviations for your file names, including as much information about a document as possible within the limits of your computer system (some systems require that you use only eight characters in a file name). File names might indicate a date ("06146.lt" or "ltr/6/14/96," for example) or might distinguish various versions of revised work ("draft 1," "draft 2") or might refer to other features you can later recall.

STORAGE.   You classify and store your files in folders or directories (depending on your computer system). Choose simple names for these folders that indicate the kind of documents they hold (letters, journal entries, assignments, reports, for example) or time periods, places where you write, or any other system whose meaning you will later remember. Folders or directories can also store other folders or directories (subdirectories); you might, for instance, keep "Work," "School," and "Private" folders in a "Fall97" folder or directory.

Note the key to your personal filing system in a handy place. Always back up your files by copying them to a storage diskette, listing their names on the labels.

2a–2 Make notes.

Word processing provides multiple ways to make and move notes within a file. Use the following guidelines for making helpful and accurate notes with word processing.

NOTE TAKING TO FORM IDEAS.   Most writers ask and answer questions as they jot notes for writing; then they draft by combining these notes with notes they've taken from other sources.

To type notes on the computer, use the normal ("default") settings in your word processing program. Use the tab key to indent paragraphs; add an extra line of space between paragraphs to make reading easier. Insert headings, especially if you have many notes, so you can search to find related ideas later.

Your ideas: Word processing allows you to write ideas as quickly as you can type. Begin typing notes without worrying about accuracy. You can shut your eyes or look elsewhere; you can turn down the brightness of your computer's monitor. Press Enter (Return) when your thinking changes direction. Press the tab key once to type a subpoint, twice for a subpoint of a subpoint.

Switch to a different font, a larger size, *italics*, **bold**, or <u>underline</u> to comment on your own ideas, as you type them. Your comments might indicate how you want to use ideas or may raise questions to answer later. Special font styles can also temporarily represent the tone you intend as you write notes.

After you write notes about your ideas, read what you have written. Reread frequently. You can return to specific words or sentences to write more, insert questions, and begin again when you have more ideas. Every time you pause, save your file using the Save command.

Ideas from reading: Take your source—books, magazine articles, and so on—to a computer when at all possible. Create a different file for source notes and name it clearly. Begin each note in the file with the bibliographic information you will need to give credit to the source in your paper.

Copy relevant sentences or passages from your reading into the file. When you react as you read, note your comments, carefully marking your language as different from the source's words. Always record the page or pages you copy from or comment on, so you won't have to find the pages again later, even if you own the source yourself (also see 7d–2, "Copying from printed sources").

Ideas from conversation: Make notes about what you have heard others say about your topic, either in conversation with you or in other discus-

2a

sions. Copy their exact words or paraphrase their comments. Identify the speaker if possible and note when and where you heard the comments. (You can later check your accuracy with any speakers you want to quote.) These notes may support your ideas or at least help you think about likely opinions about your topic.

Keep notes from conversation and organized discussions of a topic together in a file. Use headings to identify the name of each person who commented on the topic and the date of the conversation or discussion.

IDENTIFYING NOTES. *Identify categories of notes:* Name your note files to show whether they record your thinking, your reading, or ideas from conversations. Within each file, include the date on which you made each note. Never use your word processor's automatic date feature for this purpose because the date will change to the current date each time you reopen the file.

You can use special formatting—for example, an asterisk or other unusual marks that may be available from your computer's Key Caps or Symbols functions—to sort through mixed sources of notes in one file. "!" might indicate notes of your ideas; "®" might indicate reading notes; "©" might indicate notes from conversation or discussions, and so on. You can search for these marks later to group ideas from related sources. Distinct marks also remind you of the kinds of citations you need to make to acknowledge your sources.

Identify your marks: As you type notes, you need to indicate specific words that are not your own. Carefully place quotation marks around passages that you copy from any source, and record the bibliographic information about the source.

If you add anything to the words you copy from printed sources, be sure to indicate what you have added. Insert "[emphasis added]" at the end of any sentence in which you underline or italicize a word or words. If you use the quotation later, you must copy it in a way that shows its original form and makes it clear that you added something not in the original.

Identify key concepts: You can format characters or words using underline, **bold**, *italics*, and various fonts to mark key concepts that you can later reorganize as you draft. Keep a list of what this special formatting means to you for later reference. (You will remove the formatting in your later drafts. Do not place these marks in language from sources without noting that they are your emphases.)

You can also search through your notes for key concepts using the Find or Search function. You can type in a key word and the computer will jump to the location of the word in your notes.

USING NOTE PADS, POST-ITS, AND NOTE CARDS. Some computers are equipped with electronic note pad or post-it options. You can open a small writing space to record ideas while you have a word processing file open.

The notes in the note pad can be cut and pasted into a document, or your writing from a document can be copied and pasted into the note pad. The material in the note pad will be saved automatically when you close it.

Note pads and post-its are especially good places to jot points you need to remember about your purpose, your readers' opinions, assignments, developing ideas, and references or citations you come across and will need to find after you close your writing.

In some computers note cards and post-its can be indexed and cross-referenced. These note card programs (such as HyperCard) are especially useful to help you remember connections when you have many sources with wide scope and variety.

Computerized note cards allow you to mark key words and phrases or insert special characters anywhere in a note and then link that note to other marked notes.

SAVING LEFTOVERS.   Keep notes at the bottom of a draft file to remind you how to begin when you reopen the file. These reminders may be progress notes, a few new lines to get you started writing again, or leftover passages from drafting that you may want to use later.

You can also insert a page break at the end of your document and place deleted passages and leftover notes on this page. When you complete a project, make a new file for these leftovers. Keep the leftovers for later changes or future writing projects.

2b Developing Ideas

You may begin to write with notes or instructions, a clear purpose, and an idea of the outcome you want. You may be writing from an already developed plan. But even without such preparation, word processing makes it easier to develop ideas.

2b–1 Answer questions.

When you begin writing, make notes about the writing situation and ideas about your topic by answering the following questions.

WHAT IDEAS DO I HAVE?   What do you know or believe about this topic? Why have you chosen it? If it is an assigned topic, what perspective on it will respond to the assignment? What would you like to learn about this topic? Are you familiar with other writing about it? Where would you look for additional information? What experiences have you had that are related to the topic and that encourage you to write about it?

Freewrite: As you start, you can try freewriting. Write without stopping or correcting errors for a set period of time; stop; read; begin again. Repeat this process two or three times. Highlight and group ideas that intrigue you; then begin new rounds of freewriting until you settle on a perspective that fits your topic and your knowledge about it.

Brainstorm: You can also quickly list every idea that comes to mind, pressing Enter after each one. Write for about five minutes and then read your list. Group all the items in the list into related categories and select items you want to develop. You can repeat this process until you have a focused list of points you want to include in a draft.

Each of these methods allows you to think as you write. When you complete either freewriting or brainstorming as a way of generating ideas, reflect for a few minutes. Pay attention to the ideas and approaches that remain clear and interesting to you. But do not settle on these first thoughts yet. They may be only a way of clearing out unconsidered fragments of thinking about your topic. Use these methods again if you find that you need to expand on a particular point or lose your train of thinking while you write.

WHO WILL READ THIS? Who is going to read your writing? Only you? One reader, a limited group, strangers? How will you judge whether your writing has been effective for these readers? What purpose will your writing serve for them? For instance, do you need to explain an aspect of your topic, inform readers of new information about it, persuade them to agree with you about it, report on studies of it, share opinions and feelings about it, or combine these goals in a specific way? What may these readers already think about this topic and your purpose for writing about it? On what basis will they judge your content and the final text you present to them?

Always identify as much as you can about actual readers and about the usual audience for specific writing situations. These answers help you decide the most appropriate stance toward a topic, identify areas where you need to add to your knowledge about it, and prepare you for your readers' questions and objections.

WHY AM I WRITING? What is the purpose of this writing? What would be its ideal effect? How will your content help readers? Your answers may change as you write, but list and focus your reasons for writing as a guide-

---

→ SECRETS OF SUCCESSFUL WRITERS ←
Finding and Developing Ideas

- Focus on your intended readers while you develop your ideas. Do you know whom you are writing for and their expectations?
- Look up key words in your word processor's thesaurus to find lists of alternative words—synonyms and antonyms—that can often suggest new ideas.
- Use Outline View to see if relationships among your materials are clear.

line when you start. These answers will help you determine the kind of document you need to produce to fulfill your purpose, to produce a suitable length, and even to decide what its printed pages should look like. Knowing your purpose helps you look for a model of a document like the one you are writing, and to better plan your time for editing and formatting.

Spend as much time as you need answering questions about your content, readers, and purpose. You can combine your answers in a separate file and then open the file to remind you of your early thinking while you draft and revise. You can keep it open on your screen to help you focus as you write. You can also copy parts of these notes to the draft itself.

2b–2 List and move ideas.

Depending on the size of your computer's memory and the limitations that places on your word processing program, you may be able to open a document file, a note pad, notes from sources, and other helpful programs, such as electronic mail, simultaneously. Learn how to move easily among open files and programs.

Reread notes you made to get started, to find the ideas about which you want to say more. Identify and list important points you want to make and subpoints that are relevant to them. Transfer to your file the list of ideas you want to include.

Rearrange items in your list to experiment with their order. Try starting the list with the idea that represents your most developed thinking. This may be a sentence that can guide your drafting. Use Copy and Paste functions to try out various sequences of ideas.

Begin again. Expand your list. Add comments and insert transitions that clarify relations between the ideas on the list. This expansion will probably stimulate other ideas. You can choose one item and add more about it, using evidence or examples from the notes under each item on your list.

If you have decided what you want to say and have little time remaining, do not rearrange your list of points or write more about them repeatedly. But try the process suggested here at least once, since your early thinking may be commonplace and will become better defined as you work. After you have summarized first thoughts that "everyone knows" and begin to think more specifically, you will find a fresh perspective.

When you have a suitable plan and have arranged your drafted notes, print a copy to see what you have written on paper.

2b–3 Think with a thesaurus.

The thesaurus in your word processing program can help you think as you write. When you are not sure that the word you have just written says what you mean, open the thesaurus to look for other words that may help refocus

your thinking. Lists of alternative words—synonyms and antonyms—
often suggest new ideas.

These lists suggest language to vary and make your written vocabulary
more precise, but their best use is to develop ideas. Do not adopt unfamiliar
words; first use a dictionary to see sample sentences so that you do not use
inappropriate vocabulary.

2b–4 Use other word processing functions to think and revise.

Lists and outlines are agents for writing, not rigid containers that fix your
ideas or their sequence. *After* you develop preliminary ideas by asking and
answering questions and inserting relevant notes from other sources, you
can use Outline View in some word processing programs to see possible relationships among your ideas. Use this function to make a plan, to rearrange
entire sections or paragraphs with one change, and to check the logical sequence of ideas. It can show where you need additional points and where
ideas need to be developed or rearranged.

If you do not have Outline View, word processing programs also often
include preformatted outline functions, so that you can easily move a list of
ideas and notes into a sequenced list of topics and subtopics. Many have
Renumber functions that allow you to renumber items you rearrange in a list.

Kept at the bottom of your draft, outlined plans for writing also help
you get started after you take a break. You can delete lines in a preformatted outline after you have written about each one and use the remaining
lines for guidance when you return.

2b–5 Make electronic and hard copies.

Some word processing programs automatically create backup copies of files
periodically. Sudden losses of your writing can occur at very inopportune
times. But if your system crashes, a backup copy will contain what you
wrote up to the last time the computer saved the file. If your program has
an Always Make Backup Files feature, turn it on. This feature may be set
to make backups at periodic intervals as well as after each time you save.
In addition, always back up files on a floppy disk before you quit writing or
turn the computer off.

Print a copy of your writing before you leave a computer that is not
your own. Print periodically when using any computer. The time and extra
paper needed to make printed (hard) copies are more than compensated by
the security of having them. If you lose your computer file, a scanner can
create a new electronic version or you can retype from the hard copy.

Reading hard copy during drafting and revising also allows you to reflect on needed changes. If you periodically print your work-in-progress,
you can return to earlier versions if you lose your direction or get reactions
to later versions that suggest a return to earlier ideas.

2c Rewriting

To rewrite a draft, try the following features of word processing. They help you reread, rearrange your points and evidence, and improve sentences.

2c–1 Reread: screens, scrolling, going back.

Experienced writers reread their writing frequently, not only to improve it but to check for connections among their ideas as they decide what to add, cut, and revise. Computers limit the amount of text you see at one time, but they compensate by allowing you to alter the text you see and move through it easily. To aid rereading, use these features.

SCREENS.   To increase the amount of text you can see at one time, try rearranging the viewing space (the screen). You can single-space your document, make its margins smaller, and reduce the text's font size. Hide any rulers, ribbons, and button bars that appear on the edges of the writing space. A "zoom" command may also fill the screen with your text.

SCROLLING.   Lines of text on computer screens move continuously as you type, to keep the point of insertion (cursor) visible at all times. But if you want to move through the text without typing, you can scroll with commands and arrow keys or by moving a scroll bar.

GOING BACK.   You can return to specific pages and find specific words or clusters of letters and symbols with Go To and Find commands. Practice these movements, demonstrated in on-screen help and manuals, and focus on a few that you want to use habitually.

2c–2 Rearrange: cut and paste ideas.

You can use the Cut and Paste functions to move text from one point to another temporarily to see how it works in different places. When you revise, keep in mind that the order of materials in your draft and the sequence of ideas in your sentences should fit the logic of your argument. Your points should also occur in the order readers expect for particular kinds of writing.

COMMON ARRANGEMENTS OF CONTENT.   Narrative writing generally contains many obvious references to time sequences, as in traditional fiction, reports, and diaries. But the most common way to sequence the content of explanatory and persuasive writing is to begin with relevant information that your readers already know and accept and then move to new points you want to make and support. Writing that makes assertions—for instance, editorials, research papers, and other analyses—first establishes a

2c

specific context, then makes a specific, limited statement, and finally supports that statement.

OLD AND NEW INFORMATION. When you read explanatory or persuasive writing, notice how it presents familiar information before unfamiliar points, both in an entire document and in each of its parts. You can identify key terms in an on-screen reading of your draft, and you can search for occurrences of the terms to check whether you have followed the pattern of building on old ideas to explore new ones.

To control the sequence of information in your writing, begin by establishing a context in which you will explore your topic. Write an introduction from notes that summarize assertions you hear, read, and assume to be true about your topic. Close this statement of context with your own assertion about it (your thesis), and then present fresh evidence that supports your assertion. In general, use this same order, from familiar to less familiar information, in your paragraphs and sentences.

2c–3 Change perspective with multiple views.

Computers provide multiple ways to see documents. You can change your perspective on the content of your writing by changing how you see the language itself. Multiple views help you see where to add, delete, substitute, and rearrange material to clarify what you have said. Read your draft periodically in one or more of the following views.

NORMAL OR DEFAULT VIEW. The Normal View of a document (the one you usually use for making notes and drafting) omits headers, footers, and page numbers. It also allows the editing commands in word processing programs to work more quickly because it makes the fewest demands on the computer's memory. The computer can move text more quickly and perform various checks more efficiently in Normal View.

Figure 2.1   Normal View

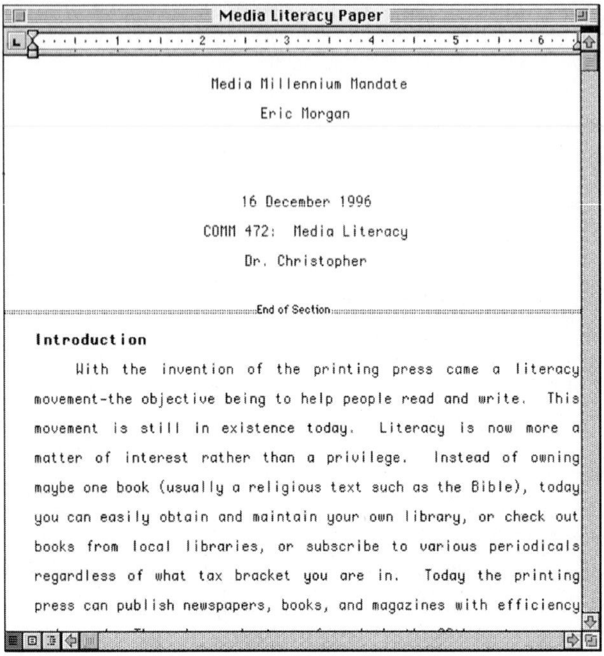

> **Media Literacy Paper**
>
> · · · · 1 · · · · 2 · · · · 3 · · · · 4 · · · · 5 · · · · 6 · · ·
>
> Media Millennium Mandate
>
> Eric Morgan
>
> 16 December 1996
>
> COMM 472: Media Literacy
>
> Dr. Christopher
>
> ·······End of Section·······
>
> **Introduction**
>
> With the invention of the printing press came a literacy movement-the objective being to help people read and write. This movement is still in existence today. Literacy is now more a matter of interest rather than a privilege. Instead of owning maybe one book (usually a religious text such as the Bible), today you can easily obtain and maintain your own library, or check out books from local libraries, or subscribe to various periodicals regardless of what tax bracket you are in. Today the printing press can publish newspapers, books, and magazines with efficiency

OUTLINE VIEW.   Use an outline of the headings and first lines of paragraphs in your document (see 2b–4, "Use other word processing functions to think and revise") or read only the first paragraph of your draft and the first sentences of each of its sections and paragraphs. Do these segments of your draft make sense as a whole? Would rearranging improve the logic of your writing? Are they clearly connected by transitions? Are their headings parallel, to indicate relationships between equal and supporting points? Outline View may help you rearrange sections of your document and change headings.

PAGE LAYOUT VIEW.   When available, a Page Layout View of a document allows you to edit, as in Normal View. But this view additionally shows and allows you to edit headers, footers, and the placement of your writing on the page. You can also see and change other formatting of your document for balance and clarity. (See chapter 4.)

Figure 2.2 Outline View

```
┌──────────────────────── Media Literacy Paper ────────────────────────┐
│  ▫ │Media Millennium Mandate                                          ▲│
│  ▫ Eric Morgan                                                         │
│  ▫                                                                     │
│  ▫                                                                     │
│  ▫ 16 December 1996                                                    │
│  ▫ COMM 472:  Media Literacy                                           │
│  ▫ Dr. Christopher                                                     │
│  ▫                                                                     │
│  ▫················································End of Section·········│
│  ▫ Introduction                                                        │
│  ▫      With the invention of the printing press came a ...            │
│  ▫      With the invention of the television came ...                  │
│  ▫ What is media literacy?                                             │
│  ▫      The phrase "media literacy" sounds nice, but ...               │
│  ▫      "Literacy" sounds a lot like literature, so it ...             │
│  ▫      "Media" is such an abstract, complex, and ...                  │
│  ▫      The means of mass communication include (but are ...           │
│  ▫ Who's interested in media literacy?                                 │
│  ▫      Even when one looks closely at the words "media" ...           │
│  ▫      The important point to make about who is ...                   │
│  ▫ When did media literacy begin?                                      │
│  ▫      Media literacy is a relatively new movement.  ...              │
│  ▫ The phrase has become so famous that it overshadows ...             │
│  ▫ The birth of the Public Broadcasting Service was ...                │
│  ▫ Where is media literacy today?                                      │
│  ▫      The problems facing media are very much aligned ...            │
│  ▫      On May 9, 1991, thirty years after his "vast ...               │
│  ▫      Another critic, Leo Bogart, states the reason ...              │
│  ▫ How is media literacy to be implemented?                            │
│  ▫      It is a monumental task to help the millions of ...           ▼│
└───────────────────────────────────────────────────────────────────────┘
```

Figure 2.3 Page Layout View

```
┌──────────────────────── Media Literacy Paper ────────────────────────┐
│                                                                        │
│        painted words being interpreted accurately? From the time the   │
│        first television sets gave America pictures of men walking on the│
│        moon and the first televised presidential debate, TV media has  │
│        grown exponentially in financial power and social influence. This│
│        paper will discuss the who, what, when, where, how, and why of  │
│        media literacy, focusing on television.  The discussion of these │
│        questions results in a mandate for the forthcoming media        │
│        millennium—the 21st Century and beyond.                         │
│                                                                        │
│        What is media literacy?                                         │
│             The phrase "media literacy" sounds nice, but being able to │
│        understand those two words is as hard as being able to understand│
│                                                                        │
│                                                   Morgan 2             │
│        any two words that powerful poets have combined.  It is definitely│
└───────────────────────────────────────────────────────────────────────┘
```

Figure 2.4   Print Preview

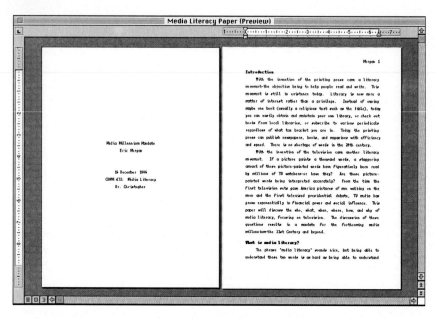

PRINT PREVIEW.   Most word processing programs will show on the screen how a document will look when it is printed. The Print Preview option may miniaturize two pages at a time across the screen, showing the relative size of paragraphs, the position of headers, footers, and page numbers, and the margins around the text. When you see noticeably long or short paragraphs and sections in this view, return to Normal View to check them. Do short paragraphs need further development? Can unusually long paragraphs or sections be divided?

2d Printing and Reading a Draft

2d–1 Read a hard copy.

You can easily miss errors or weaknesses in your draft when you read on the computer screen. Read a hard copy of your draft to determine the flow of its points and to catch obvious errors. Then read it again more carefully, marking the changes and corrections you want to make and places where you think substantial change, expansion, and editing are needed. Note sections to cut or move.

2d–2 Ask for help.

When you have time before your deadline, take advantage of it by asking a skilled reader to read your printed draft. Ask for both a general reaction and specific places where your reader has questions, sees typographical errors, or can offer suggestions. Always tell a reader the elements of the writing situation: your purpose, potential readership, your approach to the topic, the kinds of sources you used, and the expected format for your final document. This information can be a guide to your reader's useful suggestions. Ask for detailed advice, not for simple praise. Always thank careful readers and return the favor.

The Next Time You Write

1. Allocate time for thinking, planning, and making changes according to your purpose, your intended readers, your knowledge about your topic, and the editing care required to reach the outcome you want in this writing situation.

2. Plan to pay more than usual attention to a feature of your writing that readers have found problematic in the past. Define this area clearly and look for ways in which word processing might help you improve it.

3. Find out how much time you devote to writing a school or work assignment in comparison to the time spent by friends and co-workers. Ask others about how they allocate their writing time for similar tasks. Do you perceive any consistent differences in the results you and they usually get? How can you improve your results?

4. If your word processing program has Outline View, open a file and view it in both Normal and Outline Views. Practice rearranging the document by moving parts of the outline, and then reread in Normal View to check the results.

5. Try reading a document on the screen, and then a hard copy. Notice the differences between your two reactions to the document. What changes to content do you want to make after you read from the screen, and then from the printed pages? Do you see more needed mechanical changes when you read the hard copy?

3

One-Draft Writing with a Computer

This chapter describes how word processing can help you meet a tight writing deadline, with very little time to develop what you want to say or to rewrite for clarity, style, and correctness. It tells how to integrate your thinking, organizing, and revising in one draft and describes steps to take to complete a final copy as efficiently as possible.

A computer can help you produce documents in one draft when you face immediate deadlines, which often occur in academic, business, and legal settings. As you undertake any one-draft project, envision your final product. If possible, review what you know about your project's purpose for specific readers and their attitudes toward and knowledge about the topic. Decide how the format and printed pages of the document should address these considerations. Determine what information you will need to discover quickly about your topic.

Attend first to production details to avoid unwelcome surprises at the last minute. Before you begin drafting, check your computer to be sure its basic features are working properly and that it is accessing supporting programs (like a World Wide Web browser, if necessary) and connections to a printer. Obtain a floppy disk for saving and transporting the file if you will print it away from the computer on which you write it. Check that a printer will be available when you need it and that the printer will print dark, even pages. Make sure you have enough of the right paper.

3a First Steps

3a-1 Establish goals.

Before you write, note your reason for writing, the identities or characteristics of specific readers, and the format for your document. Find a model document written for the same purpose and readers if possible. Use it as a guide to approximate length, to an approach you might take, and to formatting. If you are writing from an assignment, review the instructions carefully and use them to organize your thinking and writing.

3a-2 Format your document.

Begin by naming and saving a file. Use the word processor's normal format or choose a font, spacing, and margins that you have determined are appropriate for the final document. Use a template supplied with the word processing program, imitate the format of a model document if you have one, or make new choices that will fit the purpose of this writing. First creating the physical appearance of your document can help you organize ideas and budget your writing time.

If you frequently encounter short deadlines for a particular type of writing, make a template—a model format—that you can use in repeated writing situations. Using such templates for essays, letters, memos, and reports will save time. (See chapters 11, "Letters and Memos," and 12, "Résumés.")

3a–3 Gather ideas.

Open your document and begin listing points you want to make, the issues that these points address, and data and reasons that support your ideas. If you already have files of relevant notes, copy the notes into the document file or open the note files for reference while you write. If you know of relevant Internet resources (such as news groups or discussion lists) or have e-mail correspondence you can use, include them in the file too. (See chapters 17, "Using the Internet for Research," and 18, "Connecting with Other Writers.")

If you are unsure of what to say about your topic, take as much time as you can to prepare. Make notes in the document as you think. A series of questions may provide new ideas. To bring to mind what you already know, you might answer the traditional Who? What? Why? Where? When? and How? questions about the topic. In addition, ask yourself what you can say based on comparisons, contrasts, a classification system, descriptions of processes, and changes over time that may have affected this topic. Obviously, such quick methods can produce shallow ideas about complex subjects, so be ready to discard trivial results quickly.

Take as much time as you can to discover and develop ideas, remembering that your first thoughts may easily guide development of your content but that they may also be obvious to readers.

3b Drafting Options

One-draft writing situations force you to focus on the final organization of your ideas at the same time as you discover, develop, and record them. Use the following guidelines to integrate your thinking and writing processes.

3b–1 Follow a model for arranging content.

If you know of a conventional arrangement for materials in documents written for similar purposes and audiences, use that arrangement as you draft your document. Make an outline based on a model document about a related topic and approach, and follow that outline to write your draft. Insert ideas and evidence from your notes.

3b–2 Follow a standard arrangement for content.

If you do not have a model to follow, arrange the materials you gather into four parts.

CONTEXT. Write a brief introduction that includes commonly accepted ideas about your topic. Begin by noting what is already known or frequently said about it. Use this introductory context to suggest that you will expand on common wisdom, oppose it, or take a new perspective on it.

ASSERTION. State your main point about your topic. This statement should close your introduction. What follows will develop, support, and exemplify your main point.

EVIDENCE. After stating your main point, begin with the evidence most frequently used to support it. Give reasons and use examples and other data that support what you want to say. Arrange the paragraphs after your assertion with the most obvious and familiar issues and information first. Then move to the most novel or controversial evidence that supports your point. Readers will be more likely to accept new ideas and arguments if you mention familiar information first.

CLOSING. Conclude in a way that acknowledges readers' possible responses to your statements and evidence. Restate your main point in a way that respects common opinions about your topic without sacrificing your assertion or credible evidence that supports it.

3c Revising

3c–1 Check continuity.

Reread your document on the computer screen. Check that each paragraph and sentence introduces the one after it and is obviously connected to the one before it. Insert transitional words and phrases that clarify relationships among sentences, paragraphs, and sections.

STANDARD ARRANGEMENT OF CONTENT

- Context: What is already known or frequently said about your topic?
- Assertion: What is your main point?
- Evidence: Support familiar, easily accepted ideas before new and controversial points.
- Closing: Conclude by indicating possible responses to your statements and evidence and by repeating your assertion.

3c–2 Review your document in outline form.

Use Outline View to check the logical arrangement of your draft. Or read only the first paragraph, the first sentences of the following paragraphs, and the closing paragraph. Does your sequence of points make sense? As you read, mark any needed rearrangements or additions in **boldface** or in brackets. Quickly change obvious errors, or boldface them so you can find them easily later.

STEPS TO COMPLETING A DOCUMENT QUICKLY

1. Spell-check the document.
2. Print a draft.
3. Note needed changes on the draft.
4. Enter changes in the file and spell-check again.
5. Use Print Preview to check for page placement, title, page numbers, and balanced length of sections and paragraphs.
6. Use Page Layout view to check formatting.
7. Make a title page if needed.
8. Spell-check *all* last-minute additions.
9. Save the document to a backup disk.

3d Rewriting

3d–1 Move passages.

Rearrange parts of the document as needed for consistent reasoning and easy movement through your points. Use the Cut and Paste commands to move material.

3d–2 Read sentence by sentence.

Reread using a grammar checker, which will show your document sentence by sentence. Unless it is obvious that the grammar checker has spotted an error of agreement, punctuation, or word choice, ignore its suggestions. Do not accept grammar or spelling suggestions unless you are sure they will improve your document.

As you read, make needed changes in the content of each sentence. Be sure that sentences within paragraphs begin with information that is already suggested or stated in previous sentences and that they end with new information that adds to the opening information. Make sure new information and emphatic words come at the end of sentences.

3e Check and Change with the Computer.

Time pressure makes it especially important to check the details of your documents carefully so your writing does not appear to have been an off-hand effort. Use the following list to ensure the best product you can achieve in the time you have.

1. Spell-check the document, but be cautious about accepting its suggestions.

2. Print a draft. Before you read it, reread your preliminary note file about your purpose and readers. Mark on the hard copy any places where your draft appears to lose sight of its purpose and audience. Mark additional changes and corrections to insert before final printing.

3. Make the changes you marked on the hard copy and spell-check the document again.

4. View the document in Print Preview. Check for attractive placement of text on pages, for a title if one is needed, and for continuous page numbers in headers or footers. Check for balance in the length of sections and paragraphs.

5. Use Page Layout view to check formatting. Do font sizes and styles, margins, spacing, indenting, and other details appear as you want them to appear on printed pages?

6. If needed, make a title page with your name and any other required information. Spell-check *all* last-minute additions.

7. Print your final copy.

8. Save the document to a backup disk.

The Next Time You Write

1. How might you plan ahead for deadlines? When you write quickly, could you begin more confidently with simple preparation?

2. Reread documents you have written under time pressure. How do their content, organization, and ease of reading differ from those you have written in an extended time? Are there recurring problems? Make a checklist for revision to use when you again must write quickly.

4

Editing Documents

This chapter describes options for editing your writing with a computer. It suggests ways to make improvements and corrections by reading a printed draft, identifying needed changes in the whole text, and then focusing on details in its parts. This process will save time and ensure that your documents say what you mean in efficient, conventional forms.

4a General Principles

Readers value brevity. Editors, teachers, general readers, and business-people often complain that documents written on a computer may ramble and be longer than their purpose requires. Such readers also want to read a document of any length as efficiently as possible. After you have written, revised, and printed a draft of a document, begin editing with some general principles in mind.

4a–1 More ideas are not better ideas.

Word processing encourages you to explore ideas because its speed and flexibility allow you to produce more text in less time than writing long-hand. On a computer you can revise your writing repeatedly, adding sentences and new paragraphs with examples and explanations. In most cases, such additions increase understanding and save your text from gaps that confuse readers.

But the ease with which you can insert new material can also encourage loosely constructed language and unnecessary repetition. Your text may say more than a writing situation requires in more words than a reader has patience to read. It may appear to be padded rather than well developed. Saying more does not automatically mean saying it well.

4a–2 Always work with a printed draft.

Editing achieves the best possible effects if you make decisions about changes on a printed copy. When you read only from the computer screen, you will miss opportunities for deletion, substitution, restatement, and other needed revisions, and you will overlook errors. You will not get a sense of the document's length and of the proportions among its parts, so you may not emphasize important points. You will also miss inconsistencies in formatting and in headings.

4a–3 Notice how local and global changes are related.

Remember that a good decision to change one part of a document may require changes elsewhere. If you modify content, rearrange large segments of text, edit the sentences in one paragraph, or change the sequence of a paragraph, look for the effect of the changes on the rest of the document. For instance, you may need to rewrite all headings in a new form or change all words related to a changed verb. Always look above and below any editing point to identify other changes it requires. Word processing programs can identify every occurrence of a word you need to edit or reformat.

4b Steps in Editing with a Computer

4b–1 Read the whole document.

Begin editing by reading a hard copy for its sense, from beginning to end, marking or highlighting any sections, passages, sentences, or words that raise questions or even slight doubts. Never ignore small quibbles about content, logic, sentence structure, word choices, spelling, spacing, punctuation, and other details. You can make the actual changes later, but at this time mark every problem you see and where you may want to make additions or deletions later as you read to mark possible changes.

4b–2 Identify global changes.

Editing involves more than changing sentences and words. After you read an entire document, make decisions about needed changes in its largest aspects—its content and consistent fit between this content and your purpose.

You may need to rewrite an introduction or reorder points that support a main idea. You may need to add examples to emphasize one or more

---

HOW TO EDIT

1. Read the whole *printed* document.
2. Identify global changes.
3. Mark local changes.
4. Insert new passages.
5. Make changes in the computer file.
6. Save deletions at the end of the file.
7. Correct errors and improve sentences.

briefly noted ideas. You may discover that you have consistently used an approach that does not fit your writing situation in one or more important ways. You may need to delete entire paragraphs, sentences, or wordy passages. Do not waste time changing details you marked for change until you identify changes in these larger, global elements.

4b–3 Mark local changes.

Mark on the hard copy any specific passages that need correction, rewriting, deletion, expansion, or substitution. Briefly identify the kind of changes you will make, for instance by using "X" near errors, "Add," "Cut," and other brief cues. Delete unnecessary words and, where you can, substitute one word for many.

Consult a handbook or expert reader to verify the need for the changes and corrections you noticed. Consult a handbook's index to find other editing points you may have overlooked.

4b–4 Insert new passages.

As you read, write on the hard copy any new sentences, clauses, phrases, or words you decide to insert. Draw clear lines that show where you want to rearrange any parts of the document that require it.

4b–5 Go back to the computer file to make changes.

Make your changes in a copy of your file, keeping an unedited version for later reference. Enter into the file any revisions and additions you've marked on the hard copy. Move sections, paragraphs, and sentences by using the Copy, Cut, and Paste commands. Always check for transitions, grammatical agreement, and punctuation around parts of the document that you move.

4b–6 Save deletions.

Place deleted passages at the bottom of the document in sequence, after a page break, where you can find them later if you change your mind.

4b–7 Correct errors and improve sentences.

Correct spelling and other errors you noticed as you read the document (see 4c–3, "Spell checkers"). Eliminate wordiness and redundancy. Eliminate prepositional phrases when you can insert their information as adjectives or in other phrases and clauses.

4c Computer Functions that Help Edit Details

After making changes from the hard copy, verify them for accuracy and clarity using the following guidelines. Again, work from global to local areas of the document.

4c-1 View proportions among paragraphs.

Paragraphs usually begin with new points or expansions of already stated ideas. Occasional one-sentence paragraphs in long documents may be effective. But in general, readers expect a new paragraph to raise a new issue and develop a point about it appropriately.

Use Print Preview to find paragraphs that are shorter or longer than others and check them to determine if they need further development, combination with other units, or division into parts. Break long paragraphs into shorter ones using the Enter key. Use Delete or Backspace to combine ineffective short paragraphs.

Print Preview can also remind you to respace lines and to avoid printing single words, phrases, and lines at the top ("widows") and bottom ("orphans") of pages. Some word processing programs can be set to automatically avoid widows and orphans.

4c-2 Improve sentences.

Computers allow you to look at a document sentence by sentence. One way to do this is with grammar checking functions. Or you can highlight each sentence and read it individually before making changes. You can also separate sentences temporarily by hitting Enter at the end of each one and carefully examining the structure and arrangement of each sentence in turn. You will not usually have time for sentence-by-sentence review of a long document. But this method is useful for editing shorter pieces and longer ones about which you have substantial questions.

Examine each sentence to make changes in the following ways.

TRANSITIONS.   Find the words in each sentence that connect it to sentences before and after it. Highlight those words to check that they create meaningful connections that accurately repeat an idea in a group of sentences or qualify what follows or precedes the sentence. Add transitional words needed to clarify relationships among ideas.

ORDER OF GRAMMATICAL PARTS.   The elements of English sentences most commonly follow a Subject > Verb > Object order. This order is not required, but aiming for it helps to reduce the length of sentences and to clarify them. Move words and phrases to achieve this order when it does not interfere with the continuity of your ideas or the context of the sentence.

Reading is most efficient when a grammatical arrangement of Subject > Verb > Object also matches the meaning of a sentence. Arrange sentences whenever possible so that the grammatical subject performs the action indicated by the verb. (Write "She fed the dog" rather than "The dog was fed by her.") Other sequences of subject, verb, and object are grammatically correct, but not always as direct and easy to understand.

GRAMMATICAL AGREEMENT. The subject and verb of each sentence must agree grammatically in person and number (*I write, she writes, they write*). If you doubt the needed agreement in a long sentence, temporarily cut and paste to put the verb immediately after its subject. A quick reading should tell you whether the two elements agree.

Check the grammatical parallelism among like elements (verbs, nouns, phrases) in each sentence. (*To eat, to drink*, and *to be merry* are parallel infinitive phrases; *to eat, to drink,* and *being merry* are not parallel.) To check agreement, temporarily move together any words that should be parallel, especially in long sentences.

Each of these editing checks treats a sentence as a separate unit. After making changes, reread to be sure that a change in one part of a sentence does not require additional changes in that sentence or in others.

4c–3 Spell checkers

Although they have limitations (such as the number of words in their dictionary), spell checkers can be useful as a final editing check. But be aware that they contain only conventional language and that some suggested alternatives may not be appropriate or correct.

WHEN TO CHECK. Spell-check a document if you wish when you pause in drafting and editing to reflect on what you are writing. Always use this tool immediately before printing. Even when you have made only a few, last-minute changes, you may be hurried and introduce errors. Recheck even very brief additions.

→ *SECRETS OF SUCCESSFUL WRITERS* ←

Spell Checkers and Grammar Checkers

- Use the spell checker frequently, to pause and reflect while drafting and editing, after completing a draft, after last-minute additions, and always just before printing.
- Always read a printed copy to check for errors a spell checker overlooks or introduces.
- Use grammar checkers only to look at sentences individually, to reflect on your content, and to catch errors.

Figure 4.1   Spell Checker (MS Word)

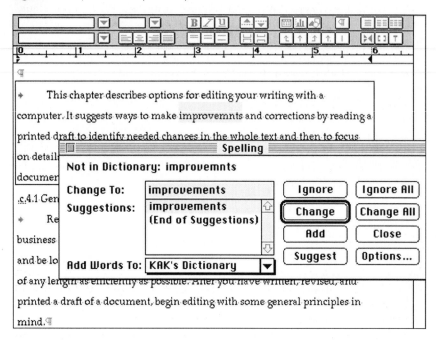

HOW TO CHECK.   A spell checker may ignore some words that you've used incorrectly. It will miss words that need capitalization ("Mr. *long*"). It will ignore words that need punctuation but lack it ("the *trees* height") and those that have unnecessary punctuation ("those *tree's* out there"). Even when you use a spell checker you must read the printed copy of your document to prevent errors like these.

THE SPELL CHECKER'S VOCABULARY.   Spell checkers have limited vocabularies. Words they stop to question may be common among the readers of your document or may be well-known specialized terms. You can make a customized spell checker dictionary by adding words that you use frequently but that aren't in the spell checker's dictionary. Always be sure that words you add are spelled correctly and will be used often enough to warrant adding to the dictionary. Adding words you make up for special, one-time uses may later cause the checker to miss errors.

4c–4 Grammar checkers

Grammar and style checkers may be built into word processing programs or purchased and installed separately. They show sentences one by one and identify words and punctuation that may need improvement. For instance, they may point out overused words and clichés, agreement errors, split infinitives, strings of nouns and prepositional phrases, and spelling errors. Some tell the average number of sentences in paragraphs and of words in sentences. They may identify the reading level of a document according to various scales of reading difficulty. Their advice and information are based on a limited, standardized, but sometimes useful understanding of grammar and style.

Keep in mind, however, that grammar checkers often identify errors incorrectly. They will, for instance, identify some sentences as "run on" when they are not. Use this function to look at sentences individually while editing, to reflect on the content of a document, and to catch easily overlooked errors. Always check their suggestions against your knowledge, examples from other sources, and the reactions of readers you trust.

4d Editing as a Help for Drafting

Careful editing takes time, but practicing it can improve your drafting habits. Editing, like drafting, may or may not achieve the results you want on the first try. You may need to, or want to, edit repeatedly, but you will eventually need to declare "time" and print your writing.

Editing can improve drafting if you keep a record of editorial changes you make frequently. In a separate file, list the editing changes you often make. For instance, you may often rearrange sentences to move verbs closer to subjects. This editing habit will indicate an element of your writing that repeatedly takes time for editing. You can watch for it whenever you edit your work. You can also copy examples from your works-in-progress into your grammar check file, naming and illustrating specific elements you change often.

As you edit other documents later, add new items to the list and make check marks after any items that often need changes. This checklist can alert you to specific problems to notice during and after drafting.

The Next Time You Write

1. Try editing on a hard copy to make a document as brief as possible without losing needed ideas and details. Then review your editing. Notice patterns, such as prepositional phrases and passive verbs whose length you repeatedly condensed. Keep these patterns in mind as you draft new material.

2. Open the file for a completed draft and view it in Print Preview. Put any disproportionately short or long paragraphs in boldface and then open

the document in Normal View to check for possible additions, combinations, and more effective ways to segment these paragraphs.

3. Read a draft with a grammar checker, one sentence at a time. Notice the changes recommended and reread sentences that the checker does not suggest changing. What disagreements do you have with the suggestions? What additional changes would you make to improve the sentences?

4. After you print an edited document, read the hard copy again. Notice the kinds of errors that remain and other improvements you need to make. Make a final checklist, indicating editing points to note before printing.

5

Formatting Documents

5a Decisions about Formats
    5a–1 Format options
    5a–2 Fit between substance and appearance

5b Templates

5c Choosing Fonts
    5c–1 Font appearance
    5c–2 Font size
    5c–3 Guidelines for choosing fonts

5d Emphasizing Text
    5d–1 Boldface
    5d–2 Italics or underlining
    5d–3 Dashes and quotation marks
    5d–4 Other special treatment

5e Spacing
    5e–1 Indenting
    5e–2 One space between sentences
    5e–3 Line spacing

5f Margins and Alignment
    5f–1 Margins
    5f–2 Alignment

5g Making Headers and Footers

5h Title and First Pages, Sections, Headings
    5h–1 Title page
    5h–2 First page
    5h–3 Sections
    5h–4 Headings

The Next Time You Write

This chapter reviews ways to control the appearance of your writing, both on the computer screen and on the printed page. Word processing requires that you make choices about formats for the size and shape of letters and blocks of text. It allows you to create visual emphasis and to vary the space around and between segments of text. Using these and other basic choices about formats, you can create a good fit between the purpose and the appearance of your writing. This chapter lists categories in which you need to make choices and guidelines for making them.

5a Decisions about Formats

In most cases, a document's appearance on your screen while you think, draft, and revise should be as simple as possible, so that it is easy to read without distractions. But after you have edited a document thoroughly, you must determine how it will look on the printed page.

5a–1 Format options

To make decisions about how to format text, both as you write and in your final printed copy, become familiar with the formatting capacities of your word processing program and your computer. You need to know what you can do with the following variables:

- Font styles and sizes
- Visual emphasis on letters, characters, symbols, and words
- Special characters
- Indentations and spaces between sentences
- Spaces between lines
- Right and left margins and text justification
- Space at the top and bottom of the page
- Drop caps, hidden text, graphics, columns, and equations

Try out the options in your word processing program in each of these categories to learn what it will do and how to do it.

5a–2 Fit between substance and appearance

Word processing allows you to create professional-looking pages with a variety of visual enhancements. Even basic programs include many graphics features—borders, frames, shadowing, and other effects.

But these convenient features may encourage you to choose formats that are more elaborate than a writing situation requires. If you create a decorated title page, make elaborate headers, and use more than two font styles and sizes for the words in a simple, brief document, this excess will make readers question your content even before they read it. However, if you do not provide a cover sheet, professional-looking styles, and consistent indentations in a report, it may look hastily assembled and your readers may question its accuracy and completeness. Fit your formats to the purpose, content, and readership of any document.

Word processing programs can also make the content of a document appear to be longer or briefer than it is. Line spacing, font styles and sizes, and added or reduced space at the top, bottom, and sides of the page can increase or lessen the mass of print on the page. But avoid the temptation to fool your readers. Readers know how well the content of a document meets their expectations. They resent misleading formatting choices, which make them skeptical about the trustworthiness and quality of your content.

5b Templates

Standardized or model formats, called templates, stationery, or macros may come with your word processing program. Use them for writing and printing standard documents. For instance, you can call up to your screen a model letter, memo, or outline that already has formats for typical fonts, indentations, spacing, margins, and so on for the type of document you need. When a particular model is not in your word processing program, you can make one by formatting a document, naming it as a template or stationery, and saving it. When you write this kind of document again, you call up the template to use as a preformatted file.

5c Choosing Fonts

Fonts are simply different typefaces such as Palatino, Helvetica, Times, and Univers. Each font has its own distinctive appearance. Your choice of a particular font should depend on print conventions that readers associate with specific types of documents. In most printed work, Times and Palatino are standard choices. (This text is printed in Modern MT Extended. Fonts like this one fit more characters per line, so they are useful for writing on printed forms and in other limited spaces.) You can make other choices for other purposes. You might print personal letters in a font that imitates handwritten script. For fun, you can write a coded message using a font such as Symbol, that substitutes special characters for keyboard letters.

5c–1 Font appearance

The appearance of a font on a screen may not reflect how it will look when it is printed. But most word processing programs show fonts accurately enough to allow you to select one for printing. Consult sample documents where possible to choose a font that fits your readers' expectations.

Fonts vary in many ways—in the horizontal and vertical spaces they occupy, in the presence or absence of decorative characters, and in options for enlarging and reducing the size of characters or adding visual emphases to characters. In addition, accented letters, symbols, or scripts that occur in languages other than modern English are not available in every font. To ease making choices, print a reference page that lists fonts by name and shows the options they include.

5c–2 Font size

The standard font size is 12 or 10 points. (Points measure the vertical space that letters and characters occupy.) For titles, section headings, signs, and announcements, you can increase a font's point size to add emphasis. But in general, use a consistent size throughout a document.

5c–3 Guidelines for choosing fonts

1. Choose Times or Palatino for professional and other public documents.

2. Follow the example of documents like yours.

3. Use no more than two fonts in a printed document—for example, one for headings and another for text.

4. Use 10- or 12-point size unless you need special emphasis.

5d Emphasizing Text

With word processing you can apply emphases (**boldface,** <u>underlining</u>, *italics*, outlining, and shadowing) to specific characters, words, or passages both on the screen and on the printed pages. Readers value effective language more than such unusual visual effects, but emphasized text is sometimes required: the titles of books, films, and other entire works, non-English words, and some trademarks require underlining or italics.

5d-1 Boldface

Use **boldface** print to emphasize the titles and headings of the sections of a document and, on occasion, to stress words that need to **jump out** to readers. Use bold less frequently in the main text than in titles and headings.

5d-2 Italics or underlining

Word processing programs allow you to insert *italics,* whereas typewriters can only <u>underline</u>. If you are printing the final version of a document, use italics rather than underlining where needed. But if your printed document will be published professionally, check with an editor about how to indicate italics.

Your word processing program may allow you to vary <u>underlining</u> with special commands. You may be able to insert <u>dotted lines</u> or <u>double lines</u> under selected text.

5d-3 Dashes and quotation marks

Most word processing programs provide options for making dashes and quotation marks.

EN-DASHES AND EM-DASHES.   An en-dash, a mark slightly longer than a hyphen, is used to separate dates, as in "1942–1943." An em-dash, which is longer than both a hyphen and an en-dash, replaces the two hyphens used for a dash on a typewriter. An em-dash sets off information within or at the ends of sentences.

Until typing these new characters becomes natural—the keystroke commands for typing them are described in your word processing manual or on the help screen—continue using one hyphen for the en-dash and two hyphens for the em-dash. You can change them in one operation with a Search and Replace function before printing.

"SMART" QUOTATION MARKS AND APOSTROPHES.   Many word processing programs have stylized single quotation marks, apostrophes, and double quotation marks (called "smart" quotation marks) that match the font rather than just vertically straight marks. You can instruct your word processing program to use "smart" quotation marks as a default.

5d-4 Other special treatment

Check your word processing manual and screen help for information about other special treatment you can apply to characters, words, or passages. You may be able to format and print selected text in ALL CAPS, in SMALL CAPS, with ~~a line that strikes through selected text~~, outlined characters, and shadowed characters. The Key Caps of some programs tell you what special characters are available in each font. You may be able to type a trademark (™) or copyright (©) symbol or accented letters (å or é).

5e Spacing

5e-1 Indenting

With word processing, making spaces with the space bar to indent text will not produce evenly aligned columns, tables, or lists. Items may look straight on your screen, but they will print unevenly. Use the following options to achieve even spacing and alignment.

TABS. Tab keys and ruler settings for tab stops control horizontal insertion positions on a screen. Set tab stops for a particular document and then use the tab key to indent and to align columns.

Some word processing programs allow you to create tables or format the text of a document in columns automatically, without using tabs. The text will appear in newspaper-like columns that appear side by side but that read ("snake") from top to bottom.

HORIZONTAL SPACING. The characters in each font occupy a certain amount of horizontal space. In "nonproportional" fonts, each character occupies the same space as all the other characters. In "proportional" fonts, the width, or horizontal space, occupied by characters varies: an *i* occupies less space than an *m*. In Figure 5.1, "Lilly" and "mommy" occupy the same horizontal space in Courier, a nonproportional font. But these words take unequal space when printed in the proportional font Palatino.

Figure 5.1   Fonts: Nonproportional versus Proportional

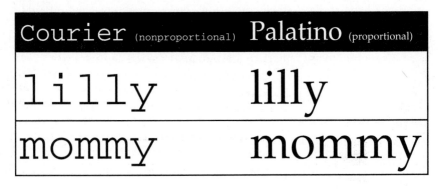

5e-2 One space between sentences

Professionally published documents use only one space between sentences and after colons, not two. Since word processing imitates the appearance of published documents in most ways, it is best to get in the habit of using one space everywhere. Until you are used to it, you can change to one space with a Find and Replace function before you print.

5e-3 Line spacing

Word processing programs can alter the space that separates lines of text, providing single spacing and double spacing as well as custom spacing. Single spacing, the default setting of most word processing programs, is conventional spacing in correspondence and documents meant to look like published print. Most headings are single-spaced.

Double-spaced documents place a line of space between lines of text. Double-spacing is standard for work projects, reports, and academic documents.

If a one-and-a-half-line spacing option is available, you can conserve paper while producing easily read print. You can also indicate custom spacing, adding, say, two lines of space between lines of text in a draft that you know will be heavily annotated in editing. (You can change back to single or double spacing for the final version.)

Remember that you should not use spacing to distort the length of a document. It is as obvious as changing font size or margins to make a text appear longer or shorter than it is.

5f Margins and Alignment

5f-1 Margins

Word processing programs have standard default margins that place one inch of space on all sides of the text. But margin requirements vary, depending on the kind of document you are producing. For instance, documents that will be bound require larger left-hand margins. Documents copied on both sides of a page require different margins for right- and left-hand pages. Texts that readers will annotate or that require editing may need more than one inch of space on all sides.

→ *SECRETS OF SUCCESSFUL WRITERS* ←

One Space between Sentences

- Use one space between sentences, not two, and one space after a colon. You can change two spaces to one with Find and Replace functions.

Other documents require other margins. Follow a model and ask readers and publishers about preferences or requirements before you print. If you have no information about requirements for a final copy or you are printing a draft, use standard one-inch margins.

5f–2 Alignment

Alignment refers to the position of the text in relation to the left and right margins. Left alignment creates even text on the left, with uneven text on the right. Left alignment is conventional in most documents and in manuscripts that will be reformatted for publication.

Right alignment creates even text on the right. It is used on title pages and to align page numbers in headers. In most books and some magazines the text is aligned on both the left and the right—this is called "full justification." Centered alignment places each line in the center of the page between the margins. Both the left and the right edges of the text are uneven. Titles and signs are conventionally centered.

Figure 5.2   Left, Right, Full, and Centered Alignment

Left alignment creates even text on the left, with uneven text on the right. Left alignment is conventional in most documents and in manuscripts that will be reformatted for publication.

Right alignment lines up text at the right. It is used on title pages and to align page numbers in headers.

Text in most books and some magazines is aligned at both the left and the right side of the page, in **full justification.** This form aligns the last character of the last word of each line of text.

Centered alignment places each line in the center of the space between the margins. Titles and signs are conventionally centered.

Your word processing program will apply these options to a whole document, a single paragraph, or a line or word you specify.

5g Making Headers and Footers

You can place uniform spaces as well as words at the tops and bottoms of all pages in a printed document. These are called "headers" (top) and "footers" (bottom). Headers and footers require separate formatting because they are actually mini-documents within a larger document. You format headers and footers individually for each document, making all the formatting choices you make about the main text. You can also copy and insert them in other documents.

Headers and footers may contain only space or a continuously visible ("running") title and page number on every page. You can format the information in the header or footer in a smaller font size or a different style, so that its reappearance on every page does not distract readers. Do not use a font size larger than the main text.

Always include page numbers on a printed document. Place them either at the upper right of a header, aligned at the right margin, or in the center of a footer. Check models and readers' preferences for the appropriate location.

5h Title and First Pages, Sections, Headings

The first formatting that readers see is the last formatting you will do before printing. It is most efficient to wait to write a title until you have completed your writing. But in addition, postpone the following choices and actions until you are ready to print.

1. Include a title page.

2. Organize a table of contents and place page numbers in it.

3. Check formats of first pages of sections and the whole document.

4. Insert headings to break a long document into sections.

5. Choose formats for borders around segments of writing.

5h-1 Title page

Many writing projects need title or cover pages. Title pages include a complete title, the name(s) of author(s), and other required information. For example, they may date the completion of the writing, state its date of delivery, or tell its purpose and intended readers. Word processing allows you to control the spacing and alignment of this information. On the cover page, the title is usually centered horizontally above the vertical center of the page. Other information may be below the title and aligned at the right margin. Consult models for guidance.

5h–2 First page

The first printed page of a document may have a different appearance from that of subsequent pages. On it, usually center your title and start the first line of text about five lines lower than it begins on later pages. Omit a page number and header on the first page of most documents. In some word processing programs you can indicate how to print the first page of the document differently from the other pages.

5h–3 Sections

Word processing allows you to write a document in separate sections and later join them in one file to format the whole document for printing. You can also separate one file into sections after or while it is written. The sections of long documents may have distinct headers that show changes in chapter or section titles yet print page numbers continuously through the document.

To decide whether to divide a document into sections, consider its length, your purpose, and the expectations readers have about similar documents. Both length and conventional formats determine whether you should use marked sections to break up your writing.

5h–4 Headings

Many writers use fewer headings than they should to orient their readers. Readers value brevity, so consider inserting headings to break a printed text into identifiable segments. Headings provide resting points, show the organization of your ideas, and make it easier for readers to return quickly to passages they want to reread.

Format headings with consistent font size and style, indentations, and line spacing for easy identification. But do not make their format so conspicuous that they overstate their presence.

The Next Time You Write

1. After editing a document, experiment by printing one page with the following visual variations:
   a. a proportional font (such as Times), a nonproportional font (such as Courier), and a font that imitates handwriting (such as Swing)
   b. a 9-point and a 14-point font size

Compare the effects. How do they change your expectations about the kind of document they might come from? Do you find each of them more or less easy to read? What kind of content might each variation be appropriate for?

2. Make a template for a kind of document you write frequently. For instance, open a new file and make a model for informal letters. Choose a font, font size, margins, and appropriate line spacing. Write an inside address that makes this document personal stationery. Use an automatic dating feature to insert a date that will change every time you open the template. Save the template file with a name that indicates what it is for and close it. Reopen it to be sure your choices have been saved in the template.

3. Open an edited document in Page Layout view. Change the right margin of the document to make the lines longer or shorter. Scroll through the document to look for any single words at the top or bottom of pages and edit or insert a Page Break to eliminate them. Add headings where appropriate and find any other needed formatting to insert before printing the document.

4. Review a few recently printed documents before formatting a new one, to evaluate the formatting choices you made for them. Apply your evaluations before printing a new document.

→ **6** ←
Printing Your Documents

6a Paper

6b Copying Options

6c Printing Errors

6d Consistent Printing

6e Color Printing

The Next Time You Write

> This chapter describes choices you need to make to print a text. It also lists ways to avoid common oversights in printing. It addresses paper choices, the appearance of a document on the page, and guidelines for completed documents.

Printing any document successfully requires that you choose an appropriate paper and determine the document's position on it, make multiple copies if you need them, and control the quality of the print. Printing a long document also requires that you check for skipped pages, uneven print quality, and inadequate or misplaced information in the headers and footers. Inattention can be costly and time-consuming.

6a Paper

Computer printers accept many kinds of paper and will print envelopes, labels, and cards. Use paper that fits the conventional appearance and formality of a document.

Check the paper capacity of the printer you use and the available paper supply so that the printer will not run out of paper before it completes printing.

6a–1 Paper size and page orientation

Determine the size of the paper your document requires. The standard size is U.S. letter (8.5″ × 11″), used for manuscripts, business letters, and most other documents. But legal documents, reports, and other documents may be printed on U.S. legal (8.5″ × 14″) or other sizes.

Text may appear on the page either horizontally or vertically. Horizontal placement is called "landscape." It prints across the long side of the page. This layout is useful when a document displays numerical data or is to be bound on its shorter side. The most common orientation is called "portrait." It prints the text vertically on the page so it can be bound on the longer side, like a book.

To vary the standard size or orientation of pages, modify the Page Setup options. View the document in the Page Layout or Print Preview option, or print one page of the document to check the results before printing all of it.

6a–2 Paper quality

Each document should be printed on paper of a quality that fits its purpose. If good impressions count, carefully select the weight, texture, and size to fit customary practices in formal writing situations. But letterhead and bond paper are relatively heavy, so they are usually unsuitable for printing long documents.

6a–3 Continuous-feed paper

Dot matrix printers use paper that is joined top and bottom. The paper has edges with sprocket holes to fit in the tractor feeder. Always remove the edges of this paper before giving a document to anyone to read. Separate the pages and arrange them sequentially.

6b Copying Options

You may find it convenient to print one copy of a document on ordinary copy paper and then photocopy it on colored or higher-quality paper. Many printers do not collate pages when they make multiple copies, and printed multiple copies are often more expensive to make than photocopies.

6c Printing Errors

Check periodically while a document is printing to be sure the printer is producing the pages you expect. Printers can run out of paper or become jammed, so periodic checking is especially important if your computer shares a printer with other networked computers. Pauses and interruptions may delay the completion of your work.

After printing, check that each page is numbered and that the margins are consistent on all the pages. Reprint missing pages.

6d Consistent Printing

Printers may make imprints with ribbons, ink cartridges, and laser processes. The quality of the latter may be comparable to that of published books. You need to monitor the consistent darkness of pages printed in any of these media.

If your printer uses a ribbon, replace it often so that the text will be dark enough to be easily read. Replace toner cartridges when the printed pages look faded. Check for consistent printing on each page and reprint unevenly printed pages.

6e Color Printing

Few documents require color printing, but color can improve the visual impact of charts, diagrams, and other graphics. It also makes some documents easier to understand. Announcements, signs, invitations, newsletters, and

6e

A LAST-MINUTE CHECKLIST

Before you leave the printer that makes the final copy of a document, check its printed pages.

1. Does each page show the needed information in its header or footer?
2. Do the pages have sequential page numbers?
3. Have all the pages been printed?
4. Is the text on each page consistently dark?

It is easy to overlook these details after writing and editing, but readers notice them as soon as they see your document.

Before you mail or deliver a printed document, check methods for fastening and covering it. If you use paper clips, enclose the document in a folder or envelope to protect it. If you use a binding or cover, be sure that it attaches all the pages of the document securely.

catalogs may be clearer and more memorable with color printing. You can print everything in color or select and print in color any pictures, graphs, numbers, or other elements of a document that need emphasis.

Color printing may take more time than black and white printing, so plan ahead. Color is becoming an affordable feature on many printers, but if you do not have access to it, you can take a file on a diskette to a copy service for printing.

The Next Time You Write

1. If your printer and word processing program will do so, try printing your document on double-sided pages. Adjust the printer's options so that information in headers, footers, and page numbers appears at equal distances from the left side of each even- and odd-numbered page.

2. Try color printing. Select titles and headings, the title page, or a graphic feature of your document for color printing. Evaluate the result. Generally, do not use excessive color or other special effects that may distract or confuse readers.

PART TWO

One Writer, Many Kinds of Writing

7

Ongoing Compositions: Records and Notes

7a Uses of Ongoing Compositions

7b Managing Record Files

7c Daily Editing

7d Notes from Sources

7e Research Logs and Storage

The Next Time You Write

This chapter tells how word processing can help you write many kinds of records and notes over an extended period and copy texts for research purposes. It offers help for keeping records of events and reflections on them, making accurate work records and logs, and writing ongoing notes of discussions and meetings. Its guidelines will help ensure that you can find specific records easily.

7a Uses of Ongoing Compositions

Ongoing documents serve many purposes. They may be reading notes kept over a short period of time, long collections of information about a special topic, personal diaries, minutes of meetings, work ledgers, correspondence, histories of research projects, lists of property, class notes, or sports data. Such records may be distributed to others or used only by their writer.

Writing with a computer makes it easy to update and maintain ongoing documents. You can easily reopen a computer file and add text, date new entries, and search the entire document for specific terms and references.

7b Managing Record Files

To ensure that ongoing records are useful over time, you need to keep them up to date and save them in accessible files. These documents require attention to other details so they later transmit the information you recorded in them. It is easy to forget the meanings of abbreviations, one-time references, and file names that make sense when you first write them. The following guidelines help manage these files.

7b-1 Keep a separate list of record files.

Make a separate document that lists the file names of ongoing documents. Include each file's folder or directory. Annotate each name with brief notes about its content and the date(s) you've entered material. You can make another list of the categories or purposes of your writing, including relevant file names in each category. This list will help you relocate files by topic.

Keep a regularly updated printed copy of this document for easy reference.

7b-2 Make templates for specific types of records.

Templates can save time when you produce ongoing compositions. (See 5b, "Templates.") To make useful templates, remember these details:

1. Name the template to classify its content—for instance, "personal journal" (or "perjour"), "English class notes" ("Engclnts"), "Min-

HOW TO MANAGE FILES OF ONGOING RECORDS

1. Keep a separate file listing ongoing writing, indicating its purposes and the dates you write.
2. Keep a printed copy of this list for easy reference.
3. Make templates for specific types of records.
4. Do not use automatic dating in templates.
5. Experiment until you find a consistent system of naming that makes individual records and their content easy to find.

utes of X Committee" ("Xcommin"), or "Project X Log" ("Xlog"). Be consistent in choosing abbreviations and list their meanings in an accessible place.

2. Use a 12-point font size.

3. Make headers with page numbers in template files.

4. Do not use automatic dating for ongoing writing. If you do, the current date will be inserted each time you reopen the file, defeating the purpose of keeping records in one file. Instead, enter a date in the file each time you add material.

7b–3 Develop a system for naming files.

Experiment until you find a consistent system that makes individual record files and their content easy to find.

Use brief, memorable codes for file names. Names can be arranged in folders or directories alphabetically or by date or title for easy recovery.

7c Daily Editing

Before you close an ongoing composition, make changes that will prevent later confusion.

1. Use Search and Replace functions to substitute complete words for abbreviations of names, places, and other information.

2. Find any words or phrases you made up on the spot and replace them with words and phrases you normally use, so you will understand them later.

3. Insert brief headings. Use **bold** or *italics* to separate topics. Headings help you search through records later. They also allow you to rearrange and group passages to write an extended treatment of a topic.

4. Format entries to make them easy to review. Use titles, headings, indented paragraphs, and page breaks.

If you need to later, you can clarify an ongoing record for other readers by adding more information and formatting. Use Outline View if available to help you group related passages.

7d Notes from Sources

Word processing helps you take notes that paraphrase, summarize, or copy sources. It helps you check and maintain their accuracy and file them for easy recovery. It makes it easy to rearrange notes and to insert their ideas or copy parts of them to your drafts.

7d–1 Making notes

Note taking is easier with computers for many reasons. If you enter notes in a computer as you read library materials, you need not recopy handwritten notes from cards or carry and reorganize notebooks. When you can, bring sources to a computer, either in their original or photocopied form. If you do first make handwritten notes, use the time when you transfer them to a word processing file to think about their content and how to use it.

As you begin taking notes from any source, record and verify all of the information that identifies it. For print sources, include the author(s), title, place and date of publication, publisher, and the title of the portion you are using—a chapter, article, or section. You can put this information in a header that will appear on every page of the notes. (See 7e–2, "Filing Research Notes.")

If you take notes while watching a film or listening to a lecture or conversation, note the name or title of the source, the speakers, actors, and producer/director/author. Include relevant information about an event, such as its sponsor and the place and date of the occasion.

Verify notes before you leave a source. You will not want to return to it later, and it may be impossible to do so. Check any content you recorded for accuracy.

When taking notes on a computer, check frequently for accidentally deleted words and passages and other errors introduced by random keystrokes. If you write while listening, use quotation marks for the speaker's exact words and use a mark of your choice to indicate when the speaker's tone affected meaning.

7d–2 Copying from printed sources

If you copy passages from a written source, verify your accuracy frequently. It is easy to omit words and lines from the source. Check for accurate recording of names and of unusual spellings.

When you copy from a source, do not change the source's words. Acknowledge errors and unfamiliar words in the source by placing "[*sic*]" immediately after them. (*Sic* means that you noticed the error and did not introduce it.) Include any emphasis from the source and place "(emphasis in source)" after it.

Insert page numbers after ideas and language you record. Indicate line and page breaks in the source if it is printed in a distinctive format. For instance, use "/" to separate copied lines of poetry so you can later divide them correctly.

7d–3 Copying handwritten sources

Copying handwritten texts requires specific care. They often contain obvious omissions and include words and characters you cannot interpret. When you encounter such problems, as you will in manuscripts and historical records, insert brackets where they occur. For instance, when a space or obvious omission is in the source, insert "[space]" in your copy. If you cannot figure out a word, either insert "[illegible]" or make a guess with a question mark. For instance, "conty" may be either "country" or "county." The context around a word may help, but record your uncertainty, for example, by recording "He lived in the conty [country?]."

7d–4 Copying from source files to your files

Some computers allow you to open more than one file at a time. You can then select text in one document, copy it, and move it to another document. Practice this process before attempting to copy source texts from disks or CD-ROM databases to your own document files.

After you create or open a document that will receive the source material, enter all of the information you need to cite it later. Then select and copy the source material and paste it directly after this information. Save your document.

7d–5 Copies from scanners

Computerized scanners copy text to a computer or a diskette. They scan a document so you can open it as you would a document you write yourself. Always label any text copied with a scanner so you do not confuse its lan-

---

> **SECRETS OF SUCCESSFUL WRITERS**
> *Verify Sources*
>
> - When you copy passages from a written source, verify the accuracy of your notes frequently. Check for omitted words and lines, precisely recorded names, and unusual spellings. Indicate all punctuation, emphasis, and formatting in your notes. Indicate line and page breaks in the source. Always check these details before you leave the source.

guage with your own. Always enter complete information about a source above the copied text so you will not forget to acknowledge its origin.

Scanners tempt writers to copy more pages than they need, so use them selectively. Depending on the quality both of the scanner and of the original text, scanner copies may introduce errors and skip words. Read them carefully and compare them with the source before you quote from them.

7e Research Logs and Storage

7e–1 Research logs

Make a computer file that is a log for each research project. List in this log complete information about every source you use. Note the date(s) when you used each source and where to find it again. This list will provide a long-term record of materials you have consulted and may want to use later in new projects. You can check it when taking notes over a long project to avoid making notes from one source repeatedly. You can also use the information in this log to make a bibliography if you need one in your final document.

7e–2 Filing research notes

Identify research notes and make files for them that you can find easily. Use the header of each document to record complete information about the source(s) included in that document (see 5g, "Making Headers and Footers"). You can later highlight and copy parts of a header to write footnotes and a bibliography.

Make folders and directories that group files related to each project. Make subdirectories that classify your notes by type of source (articles, books, events), by place and date, or by other memorable categories. A good filing system and a separate research log save time and prevent loss of materials.

The Next Time You Write

1. Read through an ongoing document looking for words and references that need clarification. Add needed headings and explanations as you read.

2. Make templates for documenting your journal, a reading log, records of expenses, or other purposes that would simplify your filing. Name these templates and store them in one folder or directory. Check their names for clarity.

3. Practice using word processing functions to insert notes from sources in an essay or another piece you are writing. Follow examples and a style manual that are appropriate for this topic.

8

Essays and Other Assigned Writing

> This chapter tells how to use word processing to ensure positive responses to assigned essays and other evaluated writing. It lists ways to control these documents so that they obviously respond to assignments. As you begin, revise and attend to details in any situation that calls on you to demonstrate effective writing, observe the reminders described here.

In writing essays and evaluated assignments for classes, training groups, and other situations, you can take advantage of word processing to improve responses from your readers. Editorial letters, articles for magazines and newspapers, and published essays must please editors. Reports to supervisors and applications to panels of judges determine promotions and acceptance to programs or positions. College essays will be graded by instructors.

The key to receiving positive evaluations of these and other kinds of assigned writing is to use a computer to help you craft a document that clearly respects its readers' expectations, time, and preferences.

8a Focusing As You Write Assignments

8a-1 Review instructions and models.

Be sure you understand the instructions for the particular writing assignment and have a clear idea of the possible ways to successfully fulfill the assignment's purpose. Follow instructions carefully, including those about a deadline. Ask questions early in the process. Envision the length, relative formality, and final presentation best suited to the assignment. Think about what your finished product will look like as well as what it will say.

8a-2 Manage your time.

Give yourself as much time as possible for evaluated projects. Plan for separate portions of time to reread, rewrite, edit, correct, format, and print. Allow for time between rewriting and later polishing so you will be able to reread edited text as critically as possible.

8a-3 Get help.

Ask for help from experienced writers as you plan, draft, rewrite, and edit (see chapters 18, "Connecting with Other Writers," and 19, "Using E-mail to Improve Your Writing"). Add notes about their suggestions and comments in the file of your draft, entering them in a distinct font to help identify them when you consider using them. Make changes recommended by your readers, but test any advice against the purpose and readership you determine from instructions and models of similar pieces.

8b Writing College Essays

Successful essays result from using strategies for exploration, questioning, and brainstorming about your topic, organizing your materials, and carefully editing your sentences. (See chapters 2, "Using a Computer in Extended Writing Processes," and 4, "Editing Documents.") Readers expect you to provide a clear main idea, to include details that make your intended meaning clear, and to back up your points with examples and other forms of evidence. Positive evaluations most often result when you focus on specific features expected in these assignments: helpful titles, an inviting introduction, a clear thesis, standard patterns of organization, and a closing that explains the significance of your essay's content. After determining your topic, gathering ideas and evidence, and drafting an essay, focus on controlling these features.

8b–1 Introductions

The purpose of an essay's introduction, which is usually only one paragraph long, is to move a reader's attention to your topic. An introduction should begin with a broad statement relevant to your emerging point, to "take in" as many readers as possible. It then gives information and examples that prepare readers for your essay's content. An effective opening addresses ideas that most people have when they consider a topic—what they often believe, consider, wonder about, or do when they encounter it.

Introductions evoke shared ideas by using one or more of the following strategies:

- Raise a problem: *Three billion people in the world go to bed hungry every night.*

- Ask questions: *What do you think will happen when everyone has access to computers?*

- Tell a story: *I remember the moment I first saw my child.*

- Begin with references to well-known statements, literary works, or facts: *Just do it.* Or *Mark Twain begins* Huckleberry Finn *by telling readers not to look for "meaning" in his novel.* Or *Federal troops won the American Civil War.*

These and other ways of framing an essay touch on a reader's existing knowledge to provide motives for engaging and understanding its content.

STRATEGIES FOR INTRODUCTIONS

1. Raise a problem.
2. Ask a question.
3. Tell a story.
4. Begin with references to well-known statements, literary works, or facts.

8b-2 Thesis statements

Readers of an assigned essay look for a thesis statement that closes the introduction. It may be one sentence or a group of sentences that specify what your essay is about and indicate the attitude and inferences you want readers to consider and accept while reading. This statement asserts your contribution to the area of interest specified in the introduction. It should indicate the result of your thinking while it forecasts your points, evidence, tone, and level of formality.

The thesis statement that readers read to help them get into your essay will often be written after, not before, you draft the essay. But you need a working thesis (a "hypothesis") as you write, to focus and organize your explorations of your topic. This working thesis will result from reviewing your notes, from freewriting, and from your first motives for choosing the essay's topic. You might, for instance, begin drafting a paper on urban development with the statement *Cities would be places of pride for their residents if they felt in control of abandoned spaces.* After drafting, as you work through your observations, data about urban trends, and examples, you might write a more specific and complicated thesis statement, like this one: *Urban development involves not only constructing new buildings in place of old ones, but making city dwellers feel that they "own" their town. Effective city management therefore includes projects, like creating parks and gardens, that give residents personal ways to renew the city's abandoned and unused space.*

This thesis is not one sentence. But it is a main idea, a clear position on necessities for developing an urban environment. It focuses a reader's attention and raises expectations about the issues to be addressed in the essay, the points that will be made about them, and the evidence and examples that will support these points.

8b-3 Patterns of organization

Readers of assigned essays look for cues about the sequence of an essay's points. Using a common pattern of organization does not necessarily simplify an essay's content or make its reading predictable and boring, especially if you have developed your ideas thoroughly as you explore a topic and write early drafts. But first thinking "I will write an alternating comparison" or "I will list a sequence of ideas as 'First,' 'Second,' 'Third' paragraphs" may well result in a mechanical, artificial sequence of ideas, not a prose that flows easily from its beginning to its end.

After you have written a draft, select and move the first sentence of each paragraph, placing them in a separate file in sequence. This list of sentences will suggest a pattern of organization that you can reinforce with transitions, repeated words, and other cues as you revise the essay. Look for patterns that suggest one or more of the following alternatives to organize a whole essay, its sections, or its individual paragraphs.

COMPARISONS AND CONTRASTS. Use comparisons and contrasts to explain and evaluate two or more events, situations, possibilities, or attitudes and to describe similarities and differences in topics that seem to be equal to each other.

CAUSES AND EFFECTS. Highlight causal connections among ideas by explaining how they result from and affect other issues. Explain the consequences of an action, the reasons for the popularity of an idea, or a conflict. Be careful not to confuse early situations with direct causes of later ones.

TEMPORAL ARRANGEMENTS. Sequence ideas by explaining their relations to each other in time. You need not "begin at the beginning" and move through time chronologically, but if you place later events and developments before earlier ones, clarify your reasons for doing so. Be careful not to confuse the order of events in time with their causes.

PROCESSES. Explain how a result has been achieved, divide your topic into its stages of development, or show a series of changes that appear to be related to a goal.

Other common patterns of organization include listing examples that illustrate a major point, explaining what a topic is *not* before explaining what it is, and organizing details as a definition of an idea.

Remember that readers of assigned essays expect you to make your organizational strategies clear, with signals that you have controlled the se-

ENSURING POSITIVE EVALUATIONS

1. Read and use successful examples of similar assignments to guide your choices of content, length, and format.

2. Choose a title that clearly forecasts the content.

3. Make your organization and logic visible.

4. Always follow conventional practices.

5. Avoid excess formatting.

6. Proofread carefully.

quence of your points. Review this feature of successful essays by moving the topic sentence of each paragraph into one paragraph, to determine if the sentences together make sense as a summary of your essay.

8b–4 Titles

An essay without a title is at the same disadvantage as a person without a name. It can, of course, contain ideas and affect others, but its identity remains hidden and it is less easy to remember and refer to later.

As with a thesis statement, however, you may want to postpone selecting a final title until you have completed revisions. A working title will help you focus and arrange your points, but selecting a final title for your writing is usually the last step in ensuring that it is identifiable and inviting to readers.

Use a word processing file to note interesting titles as you encounter them in other writing and to experiment with ideas for the title of a specific piece as you work on it. Your titles may allude to other works by changing elements of common phrases: "Tar and Peace: Road Construction after the War." They may be descriptive: "Reading and Rereading Coleridge's Poetry." Choose brief titles that fit the content and attitude of your essay without promising readers more or less than it includes.

8c Revising for Positive Evaluations

The following suggestions are especially important if your writing is to be evaluated for a grade or will determine a decision about your future.

8c–1 Follow examples.

Find successful examples of similar responses to assignments. Ask the person who assigned this writing and other writers for models, or read published examples to see strategies you might adapt. Use these examples to help you format your response to the assignment.

8c–2 Check your essay for ease of reading.

● Does its title clearly forecast the content?

● Are the organization and logic visible?

● Readers of assigned writing appreciate visible cues about its patterns of development. If the directions and examples do not exclude them, add headings and subheadings to make parts of a document easy to distinguish.

● Are the length, appearance on the page, and formatting details conventional for this kind of writing?

8d Checking and Rechecking for Quality

8d-1 Avoid excess formatting.

Review choices about formats that might interfere with reading. Excessive mixtures of fonts and sizes, numerous indented subheadings over brief paragraphs, and more than a few emphasized characters and words are all distracting. They suggest that you paid more attention to a document's appearance than to its content.

Check for your title at the top of the first page. If a title page is requested, prepare one, but if it is not, do not add one (see 5h, "Title and First Pages, Sections, Headings"). Readers prefer that you do not add extras.

Add headers to each page that include a title and page numbers (see 5g, "Making Headings and Footers"). If you have doubts about how a document should look, ask for more information about the assignment.

8d-2 Proofread carefully.

Take time to reread for errors in printed pages. Follow these steps:

1. Read the document slowly after printing an edited copy. Check it for suitable content, precise language, headers and spacing, and conventional grammatical and mechanical forms. Test suggestions from a spell checker and grammar checker against dictionaries, handbooks, and your own knowledge. (See 3d–2, "Read sentence by sentence.")

2. Proofread by reading one sentence at a time, starting at the end and moving to the beginning of the document. Transfer changes and corrections to the document file. Spell-check last-minute changes.

3. Reprint the document.

4. Check that the print is dark and uniform on each page.

5. Use a paper clip to attach pages unless other methods are requested.

The Next Time You Write

1. Begin assigned writing by reviewing the assignment, making a plan for your time, and gathering all the sources you will need.

2. Allow time between first completing your assignment and going back to recheck all its details. Notice how this distance changes your assessment of what you wrote.

9
Research Writing

9a Local Computerized Searches for Sources
    9a–1 First steps
    9a–2 Computerized library catalogs
    9a–3 Conducting searches

9b Specialized Computer Databases and Electronic Sources
    9b–1 The form and content of databases
    9b–2 Searching databases
    9b–3 Other database resources

9c Obtaining Sources You Need
    9c–1 Requesting electronic texts
    9c–2 Copying electronic texts
    9c–3 Checking and citing electronic sources

9d Making Notes from Sources

9e Writing Specialized Parts of Research Documents
    9e–1 Annotations
    9e–2 Abstracts and summaries

9f Formatting Research Writing
    9f–1 Guidelines for formatting
    9f–2 Word processing help for formatting

The Next Time You Write

This chapter addresses how computers and word processing ease three important processes of research writing. It tells how to search computerized catalogs in libraries to survey available sources. It explains how to obtain and cite electronic sources. It also suggests guidelines for presenting research in printed documents. Word processing helps format source citations and makes it easier to write the specialized parts of some research documents: footnotes, bibliographies, summaries, and abstracts.

Doing research is a way of thinking about any topic or problem. The essence of writing from sources is that your ideas evolve and change in light of new information. Consequently, you need to remain flexible throughout any research project, and computers allow you to do so. In addition, computers and word processing can become your partners as you prepare the specialized parts of research documents.

Computers can help you complete school, business, and personal research projects in many ways. They encourage you to develop new angles on a topic for writing as you discover, gather, and record information in lists of sources. They allow you to read sources from a computerized database, copy them to your own files, and order copies from publications. They improve note taking by making it easy to record accurate information about a source, copy or summarize the source, and transfer notes to your draft document. They also help store notes so you can find them later. They allow you to write sections of a research document and join them, rearrange them, and keep their progression clear with numbered headings and titles as well as make tables of contents automatically for sections and entire documents. They also make it easier to prepare specialized elements of research documents: lists of works consulted or cited (bibliographies) and footnotes or endnotes. They make it easier to write abstracts and summaries by allowing you to delete and add material from your own and others' work.

9a Local Computerized Searches for Sources

Specialized library online catalogs have replaced printed card catalogs and have simplified access to sources. These online catalogs allow you to search local and distant libraries and preview the content of some sources they list. Research computers in local libraries may provide indexes to sources, find abstracts of articles, and allow you to print entire articles or books.

9a-1 First steps

You first need information about a library's available computer resources and how to use them. Ask for help at the reference desk. Are there any handouts or books that explain what is there and how to use it? Are classes offered? What computer resources are related to your specific interests, for instance in government reports or literature? Be persistent in asking questions. It takes time to learn conventional ways of talking about new systems.

Library staff members and experienced friends will help as you begin to use computers dedicated to finding sources. After you know what is available, learn the computer commands needed to find and view information. (See chapter 17, "Using the Internet for Research," about searches and importing sources.)

9a-2 Computerized library catalogs

Computer terminals that conduct searches through library catalogs have almost universally replaced card catalogs. New online catalogs show records of all the materials in the library, including books and journals. Libraries give them nicknames like MELVYL or UNIS. When you view the terminal, the first thing you will see is instructions about searching for materials. These instructions tell you how to enter information—author names, titles, topics and key words—to conduct a search.

Online catalogs and other search computers require that you be accurate when entering search terms. Authors' names, titles, and key words must be precisely spelled; the computer will respond to any misspelled or omitted words with error messages or information you may not want. When this happens, reenter the search information correctly. If you get stuck, ask for help. Don't give up. Online catalogs are the only way to find sources in many libraries.

HOW THE CATALOG WORKS. Spend time trying out searches for material listed in an online catalog. Practice using the commands on the terminal screen, which tell how to move from one kind of information to another. For instance, you may see an index of authors' names or topics and need to move forward and back within it. You may want to move from long to short views of information about books. The screen information will tell you how.

When you find sources that may be useful, make a note of appropriate information about them. (Some library terminals are connected to printers that will print the information from the screen.) You will need all of the following information to find a source or request it if it is checked out or kept in a special collection or in another library.

Figure 9.1   Online Catalog

```
                                                    U of U Libraries Catalog
                                                               Introduction
--------------------------------------------------------------------------
                          Welcome to UNIS!
               University of Utah Libraries Catalog
                         SEARCHING UNIS

For searching:        Examples:                    Search online help type:
  AUTHORS               a =hawking s                   exp a
  TITLES                t =journal of psychology        exp t
  KEY WORDS             k =arts and censorship          exp k
  SUBJECT              s =winter olympics               exp s
  CALL NUMBER          c =hf296c53                      exp c




                  Type command and press  <ENTER>
                  Other online help press <ENTER>
------------------------------------------------- + Page 1 of 2 -------------
                  Enter search command              <F8>  FORward page
                  NEWs


NEXT COMMAND: ▌
```

1. Call number

2. Author

3. Title

4. Location in the library

5. Is it checked out? When is it due?

Online catalogs sometimes also tell you more information—a book's number of pages and whether it contains an index and bibliography, for instance. The call numbers of the source can also help you search for related materials.

SPECIAL COMPUTERIZED CATALOGS.   Some specialized library computer terminals are dedicated to accessing the catalogs of other libraries. When a library has such terminals, they are usually for nearby collections that you can visit or from which you can request and receive materials relatively quickly.

9a–3 Conducting searches

Computer catalogs and indexes quickly show a wide variety of sources. But they produce results only in response to terms that you enter to guide searches. To discover material relevant to a topic and develop or narrow

Figure 9.2   Online Catalog Record

```
Search Request: A=TWAIN                      U of U Libraries Catalog
BOOK - Record 415 of 640 Entries Found                    Brief View
-------------------------------------------------------------------
Author:        Twain, Mark, 1835-1910.

Title:         The complete adventures of Tom Sawyer and Huckleberry Finn
Edition:       Centennial ed., 1st ed.

Published:     New York : Harper & Row, c1978.
-------------------------------------------------------------------
LOCATION:            CALL NUMBER            STATUS:
LC BOOKS, LEVEL 4    PS1303 .A3 1978        Charged, Due: 02/27/96




-------------------------------------------- Page 1 of 1 ---------------
STArt over      LONg view                    <F6>  NEXt record
HELp            INDex                         <F5>  PREvious record
OTHer options   GUIde

NEXT COMMAND: █
```

your earliest ideas about what you need to know, you must stay open to rethinking the categories you first choose to look for information. For instance, entering the search term "writing" might produce no results or,
more likely, too many sources. You could next try related but different
terms—"composition," "scribe," and "publishing" might produce better
results. You can also slim down a broad topic by adding words to your
search: "writing and computers and research" as a three-word search could
locate the book containing the material you are reading now.

Think of online searches as ways to explore an idea or interest, not to
find support for a fixed vision of it. Move to a new problem or focus if various searches continue to provide too little or too much information.

In addition, remember that the terms ("key words") that you think will
locate materials may differ from the key words used by online catalogs. The
terminal makes general suggestions about how to search with key words,
and some systems have a reference book that lists key words. Use various
forms of words, synonyms, and terms that broaden and narrow your topic.
Try a thesaurus for finding related terms. Skim one source for terms, approaches to a topic, titles in its lists of references, and the names of people
who write about it to find words to enter in a search.

9b Specialized Computer Databases and Electronic Sources

In addition to catalogs, library computers allow you to find specialized lists of sources, abstracts of articles or their entire texts, encyclopedias and dictionaries, pictures, and audiovisual sources. When these computerized sources are available, you can find them only at specialized terminals.

9b–1 The form and content of databases

Computerized lists of sources will help you make lists of articles in journals, magazines, and other nationally and internationally published periodicals. This specialized computer information is stored in databases, which are available on CD-ROMs. You view these databases from networked research terminals, or you place the CD-ROMs in a drive connected to a terminal.

Electronic periodical indexes are named and classified by the field of interest they cover. For instance, MLA and ERIC are names of databases related to modern language studies and to education, respectively. GEOREF is a geology source; Chemical Abstracts lists articles about chemistry and summaries of their contents.

Your library will have a list of available databases. In general, the databases contain up-to-date information. They index sources and documents across many popular and specialized topics. Databases may include telephone directories, business and entertainment information, government patents and trademarks, and many other areas of information.

9b–2 Searching databases

Computer terminals that display databases work much like online catalogs. They search for an author's name, an article's title, or search terms (key words). Some databases contain entire texts and some show what has been written about a topic in a specialized field.

To begin, choose search terms made up of words that focus your topic. Use more than one word to prevent your search from turning up too extensive lists. For instance, in BIOSYS BIOLOGICAL ABSTRACTS you might start with "cell," which would produce a long list of sources. To narrow the search, you might add "human" ("cell and human" is the required form). Additional terms would further condense the list of sources that the database finds. "Cell and human and fetal and alcohol" would locate articles about fetal alcohol syndrome.

You should mark the entries you may want to use as you read the search results. Follow directions to mark all that even vaguely interest you. You can discard useless sources later.

Figure 9.3 ERIC Database Search—"Writing"

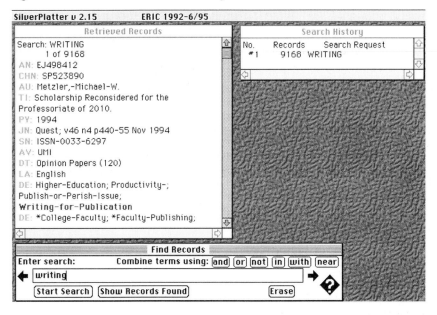

Database search results first list the most current works, followed by older ones. You can thus see current approaches to topics that may disagree with or build on older work. A useful way to understand accepted ways of thinking about your topic is to look first at an example of recent work; you can get a sense of current terminology and identify influential earlier sources that may appear later in the source list. Then look at earlier work, to see how the conversation about a topic has set new questions, changed direction, and evolved, perhaps as a result of new methods for gathering and interpreting data.

Never quit a database without giving it the precise instruction you want it to follow. For instance, you will lose your current search list if you do not request that it be printed before you move to another database or another search. Always check the possibilities on the monitor and select one that will keep search results so you will not need to repeat the search.

If your search terms do not turn up useful sources, read an article or a few abstracts related to your topic. Find key words in the article or abstract and search again using those. People who identify search terms for a particular database may be computer specialists who are not specialists in the subject they index. In addition, search terms vary from one database to another, even among those in related fields. Keep trying new terms.

9b–3 Other database resources

In addition to making lists of sources, databases may provide materials themselves. Some databases include text, pictures, film clips, and audio files. For example, a multimedia encyclopedia will not only tell you about an anaconda but will include a picture of one and show a short video clip. These sources multiply the contexts in which you receive information, so they help you explore a topic from multiple perspectives. You can sometimes move information from a database to your own note files (see 7d–4, "Copying from source files to your files").

9c Obtaining Sources You Need

Databases contain specific names and descriptions of articles, books, and other materials, or they contain the materials themselves. Online catalogs simply tell what a library owns. After you have a list of sources from a database, you need to check for their availability. Go back to your library's online catalog to see if it has sources you want and if they are available or on loan.

If your research must be finished quickly, you probably will not have time to request a source through the interlibrary loan department of your library. If you can wait to get the source, supply that office with all the information it requests. If you wish, you can use online catalogs and Internet searches to discover the locations of libraries that have sources you need. (See chapter 17, "Using the Internet for Research.")

9c–1 Requesting electronic texts

If you want a specific article that you find in an electronic database, check the instructions that appear when you close the database. Do they ask if you want to receive a copy? Some will ask if you want to print one document from the computer's screen or if you want to print all the articles a search has listed. Your library will probably charge for these copies.

Some databases include a command allowing you to ask for a fax copy of one or more articles. If so, you will need to enter a fax number where copies should be sent. Your library will charge for this service, or the database may request a credit card number to pay for fax delivery. (Sometimes these requests do not work, for a variety of reasons. Do not count on them if you are in a hurry.)

9c–2 Copying electronic texts

In addition to lists and descriptions of sources, computerized databases contain encyclopedias, large dictionaries, well-known literary and other texts, and many other kinds of data. As you read these CD-ROM sources, the terminal will show command choices. You may print portions of the text at a printer attached to the computer or save a copy on a diskette. Treat these copied passages as you do scanned material (see 7d–5, "Copies from Scanners").

9c–3 Checking and citing electronic sources

ACCURACY OF ELECTRONIC SOURCES.   If you copy information from documents or entire passages from texts in databases, verify the accuracy of the electronic texts. You may want to read a work first as it appears on the database while you are there since it is more convenient to do so. But remember that some electronic versions of written texts, especially well-known literature, have been edited in ways that change their words and emphases. If you change the language from a source after you check it against an accepted printed text, cite the source you use, not the electronic one. If you use only an electronic source, refer to the specific database or network site where you found it.

CITATIONS OF ELECTRONIC SOURCES: EXAMPLES.   The following are examples of ways to cite electronic sources. To determine the precise form of citations, always use the most current manual of style used by those who write in the field of your topic. These examples indicate how to proceed when you cannot find other examples. (See chapter 21, "Writing for the World Wide Web," for explanations of the terms, abbreviations, and addresses used in these examples.)

General form: Use this form for a text cited in a list of sources.

Author's Last Name, First Name. "Title of Work." *Title of Complete Work.* [computer address] [path] (date of message or visit).

Text published on networks: Use this form for text that you retrieve with Internet connections from World Wide Web pages, Gopher sites, and direct file transfers (FTP sites).

Kehoe, B. P. (1992). "Zen and the Art of the Internet." (2nd ed.) [Online]. Available WWW: http://whatever.the/address.would/be.html. (the date you found it).

U of Michigan English Department. "Teacher Resources" [Online]. Available via Gopher: machine.name/directory/directory/ (The "last revised" date or the date you found it).

E-mail and news group messages: Cite these as personal correspondence.

Flood, Tim. "Re: why we teach composition." 17 April 1995. Online posting. Megabyte University (mbu-l@unicorn.acs.ttu.edu).

Kolko, Beth. "Wyoming paper proposal." E-mail to the author. 5 April 1995.

Wilson, Kim. "Re: the continuing crisis." 22 April 1995. Online posting. News group comp.edu.composition. Usenet. 23 April 1995.

9d Making Notes from Sources

Successful research depends on careful note taking. Word processing makes it easier to make notes and to copy from printed sources and handwritten manuscripts and allows you to make direct copies with scanners. You can create files of notes that can be combined, moved directly into your research document, and filed for later uses in new projects. When you make notes for research, be sure to decide ahead of time how you will organize them and identify sources systematically, so that you will not become confused about how to find materials you have noted or whether you have already consulted them. For details about taking notes from sources, see 7d, "Notes from Sources."

9e Writing Specialized Parts of Research Documents

9e–1 Annotations

Annotations are brief notes that summarize your opinions about your sources. With word processing you can easily insert them in your note files, perhaps to say why and how you will use a source. You can indicate that the annotations are yours by placing brackets around them. The Table function of your word processing program may allow you to write annotations on the sides of pages. (Check on-screen help and a manual for directions.)

Annotations on notes may identify out-of-date sources and criticize their logic, their writing, or misstatements of fact. They may be cross-references to other sources, indicating disagreement or agreement between them. You need not agree with a source for it to be a valuable contribution to your research.

Writing annotations helps you begin drafting claims you want to make in research writing and prevents source material from overwhelming your plan for writing. You can transfer annotations to your drafts with a reference to their origin. Use consistent marks to separate these comments from quotations and paraphrases of sources.

9e–2 Abstracts and summaries

An abstract condenses a document you write so others can grasp its content quickly; it might appear at the beginning of an article or report or in a database that lets others see at a glance what you wrote. Summaries of your own or someone else's writing are needed in many places—examinations, research writing, and reviews of literature in reports and elsewhere. You write an abstract or a summary after you read or write a longer piece. Word processing saves you time by allowing you to combine selections from a long document and then edit them for these purposes.

WRITING AN ABSTRACT.   Make a copy of the file containing your original document. If your word processing program has Outline View, use it to move headings and the sentences immediately following them into one file. Then return to Normal View to edit this list of statements so that it represents your thoughts in the longer document in brief form.

If your word processing program does not show outlines, highlight and copy headings and first sentences. Then paste them into a file you have created for your abstract. Edit the sentences to represent your thoughts in the longer document in brief form.

Abstracts need not include transitional words. Their form and the title "Abstract" tell readers that they condense a longer document.

WRITING A SUMMARY.   You can include in your research document a summary of your own ideas or of the ideas in someone else's work. Writing a summary takes more time than writing an abstract because the material to be summarized may not be available in a file for transfer and may not be easily scanned. If it is, use the procedures for writing an abstract. However, summaries need transitional words to show the purposes and logic of the original. If you use a summary of someone else's writing in your own final document, remember to acknowledge the source of the words you copy.

To summarize material in printed form, first make a copy of it. Write the summary by using one of the following options, or combine a few of them.

● Highlight the important points made in the document. Copy these highlighted elements, in sequence, to a new computer document. Create one continuous summary, using transitions to make connections between ideas clear.

● Bracket the portions of the document that you need to summarize its content. Using these bracketed sections as a guide, draft in a new computer file a brief statement of the points they make. Edit your restatement for continuity.

● Cross out material in the original that can be omitted without losing or distorting its relevant points. Copy the remaining sentences to a new computer file. Rewrite them as a continuous statement in your own words.

● After reading the original, list the points from it that you want to include in a summary. Paraphrase these points by using alternative word choices, rearranging sentences, and restating the evidence that supports them. Then edit this paraphrase so that it summarizes the original in your own words.

You need not use "the author says" or make other explicit references to the source if you footnote it in your longer document.

9f Formatting Research Writing

In general, follow guidelines for evaluated writing (see 8c, "Revising for Positive Evaluations") to prepare a research document for printing. But when formatting the document, remember two further qualities:

First, research writing uses the language of its sources, in quotations, paraphrases, and discussions of other people's writing. It shows how your thinking depends on and contributes to a conversation about your topic.

Second, the format of a research document highlights its sources, in notes and bibliographic lists. It helps readers verify the accuracy and scope of the sources you used to support your contribution to an ongoing discussion of the topic.

9f-1 Guidelines for formatting

The formatting of a research document depends on customary requirements in the community of researchers in your field. Three considerations will help you format particular research documents.

The specific purpose of your document: Is it to be the basis for a decision or an action that requires expert advice? Is it a term paper, a dissertation, or a brief assignment? Is it to be published, and, if so, in what community will it be read? Format to make your research writing fulfill its purpose, following conventions for these and other situations precisely.

The stated preferences of its intended readers: Were you asked to write according to conventions in a specific style manual by a teacher, adviser, editor, or person who will use your research in making a decision? Do your readers often read documents like the one you are writing and expect yours to imitate them? Follow an example that your readers are familiar with.

The subject and methods of your research: What do specialized style manuals tell you about page formats and citations of sources in the writing about this subject area? Follow their advice precisely.

Think of the formatting conventions for research documents as directions to you. The order, punctuation, and special characters used for quotations and citations within your document, in its notes, and in the list of sources at the end must meticulously follow the style guide specified or required by your readers. Every detail of a citation, including the spacing between words and location of punctuation marks, must be exact. It is better to copy from examples in a style manual than to memorize the forms. Never guess, always check. (See "Additional Sources" on page 185 for a list of style manuals for various fields.)

9f–2 Word processing help for formatting

CITATIONS. Many standard formats for research documents call for citations in parentheses within the text, either after a first complete reference in a note or for all citations. But in some disciplines, references are made in footnotes or in notes at the end of chapters or sections (endnotes). In still others, however, notes and references appear at the end of an entire document.

Word processing makes it easy to place citations in required places. Functions in many programs will add footnotes and endnotes with simple keystrokes. These functions, which may be Insert commands, allow you to write the notes in a separate area on the screen; they are then listed with numbers or other identifying characters either at the foot of the page or at the end of the chapter or document. The notes are automatically moved, deleted, or renumbered if you move, delete, or rearrange text they are attached to. Some programs will change footnotes into endnotes so you can see your citations while you draft and edit and then relocate them before printing.

If you make notes manually, write them immediately after the number or symbol at the end of the passage they refer to. After drafting and revising, move the notes to the bottom of the pages where their reference marks appear or, more easily, place them in a list at the end of the chapter or document.

You can transform notes into entries for a bibliography by editing each note to fit the required bibliographic format. Some word processing programs can sort lists alphabetically. Check your manual for options.

MERGED SECTIONS OF RESEARCH WRITING. You can write long research documents in sections and then move the sections into one file or join them with an Insert File (or Print Merge) command. This command will apply sequential page numbers, headers, and footers throughout the longer new document (if you have defined them in the original documents). You can also make tables of contents and indexes automatically after you complete a document. These lists will include references to page numbers where marked headings and indexed words appear. Make these reading guides just before printing.

INDENTED QUOTATIONS. Word processing makes it easy to set off quoted lines of poetry, long passages of prose, figures, and other data. Some word processing programs will indent the margins of these segments of text if you create a "style" for them in your word processing style list. (You might call the style "Indents.") Whatever system your word processing allows, set the margins for indented material an inch wider than the standard right- and left-hand margins. Use the same line spacing and font size for indented material that you use for the entire document.

The Next Time You Write

1. Choose a topic you are interested in and go to a local library or information center to find available sources about it by using a computerized catalog. Ask for help; read instructions; ask for more help. Practice using the online catalog until you are comfortable doing so.

2. Look for a particular book, article, or newspaper in a computerized catalog. Experiment with entering author names, titles, and subject terms until you find the source. If you cannot find it, ask for help; it may not be in your library at all, or you may have missed an important cue to finding it.

3. Undertake a search for sources of information on databases in a library. Spend time using various key words and search terms; review the variations on the terms to see which terms produce results you want. Try this with a variety of topics so you become familiar with varying search terms to narrow, broaden, and modify the scope of a topic.

4. Find a published research report or academic paper. Read it carefully to notice its uses of sources, how it cites them, and how it lists or does not list them as a group. Does this document agree with its sources, disagree, or attempt to build on them? What cues does it give about its attitudes toward its sources?

5. Practice using your word processing program to insert notes about sources in an essay or another piece you are writing. Follow examples and a style manual that are appropriate for this topic. Try making a table of contents and an index for this document. Edit both for clarity, checking their entries against the page numbers of your document.

10
Reports

This chapter describes common types of reports, explains the sections they usually include, and shows how word processing can help groups and individuals write them, format them easily, and include visual presentations of the information they contain.

A report is a specially formatted document that explains investigations of a problem or the status of a situation. It usually includes an analysis of research results and of the situation it describes and explains methods that led to its conclusions or recommendations. It may list questions or problems a group has addressed and tell specifically how it addressed them. Reports are often written by more than one person for the specific readers who assigned them, but they may also be periodically required information that monitors an organization or activity. A yearly financial accounting and the President's annual State of the Union address are both reports that deal with specific topics every time they are written.

10a Types of Reports

There are many types of reports. Status reports tell "where we are now and how we got here" and explain expected future actions or developments in a situation. They may concern the finances of a company or the ongoing development of a project.

Research reports may argue for a thesis, present new knowledge, or take a position that will contribute expertise to making a decision. They clearly state the sources of their conclusions. They usually also include a narrative of the research activity that led to their main points and suggest further study.

Informative business, government, and other group reports usually include the steps that the writers have taken to address a problem. A committee report, for instance, usually combines a record of the committee's activities with plans for the future and recommendations to the group or person to whom it reports.

10b Typical Sections of Reports

Reports often have conventionally titled and separated sections. Their purpose is to help accomplish the report's goals and support its credibility. Depending on their purpose, length, and formality, reports may omit some of these sections or combine them, with or without labels or headings.

10b–1 Statement of the problem

Many reports begin with a statement of the problem or a descriptive section that establishes the context in which the report was written. Like the introduction to any composition, this section supplies background information about why the report uses a particular approach to the topic or why the specific instructions to write it were given.

10b–2 Findings

Reports next state their findings, which may be called "Conclusions" or "Results." This section may include recommendations for action, or recommendations may be listed in a separate "Recommendations" section.

Findings and recommendations are always stated early in reports so that their readers do not need to search for them.

10b–3 Review of the literature

Reports may include a "Review of the Literature" section that summarizes previous writing on the subject and relevant activities others have undertaken. As in other compositions, this section reviews the sources of arguments that both support and differ from those in the report.

10b–4 Methods

A "Methods" section explains the procedures used to gather information. It shows how research and observations were conducted. For instance, in technical and scientific communities, a methods section indicates the standard that was used to evaluate experimental data or the system of verification that was applied to statistics and measurements. But even without such explicit information about the "tests" applied to information you gather, you should explain why you used the methods you did, so that readers know that the report's conclusions are based on the best possible evidence.

TYPICAL SECTIONS OF A REPORT

1. Statement of the Problem
2. Findings
3. Review of the Literature
4. Methods
5. Case Studies
6. Discussion

10b–5 Case studies

A report may include one or more case studies in a separate section, to expand and clarify the reasoning and conclusions in other parts of the report. Case studies also may be the basis of an entire report. They narrate long-term observations of people and other phenomena related to the report's topic. Darwin and Freud, for instance, reported studies of individual cases to establish their theories.

10b–6 Discussion

Reports usually include a "Discussion" section that assesses the relationship between the data reported and the report's findings. It may present arguments about the issues at stake in its recommendations, suggest alternative interpretations of data, or compare the report's results to those in previous studies.

10c Guidelines for Writing Reports

Reports differ in their tone, approach, and the length of their sections, so use models and handbooks to help you control these features and determine the separately headed sections you should include. The following guidelines will help you take advantage of word processing to write reports.

Taking notes: As you collect data and other information, follow guidelines for taking research notes (see 7d, "Notes from Sources"). If you are working with a group to gather information, decide together on a standard format and procedure both for naming files and for titling documents and organizing their information.

Keeping logs: In addition to making notes from sources, keep ongoing logs describing all the activities you undertake (see 7b, "Managing Record Files"). This log may record individual actions and minutes of group meetings. It may list sources, dates and places you investigate them, and names of people, documents, and materials you consult. If you are conducting experiments or dividing work within a group, carefully note each action taken and who took it. You may need this information for future reference and verification.

Drafting the report: When it is time to draft the report, divide its writing into sections. If you are working with others, you may want to assign separate sections to individuals for drafting (see 20a–2, "Assigning tasks").

1. Begin by writing the Statement of the Problem, to clarify the purpose and expected outcome of your report as a guide to writing it.

2. Write a Review of the Literature to review previous discussion about your topic. Or write a section in which you narrate the actions

and circumstances that led to the current situation you are describing. Highlight, copy, and insert in this section information from your notes, logs of discussions, and other activities. Cite information about sources fully and acknowledge uses of their language.

3. Write the Methods section of the report. As in the Review of the Literature section, insert information from your log of activities in your files of notes from sources. A Methods section is a narrative of procedures. It tells how particular ways of gathering information produced your results. When results rely on statistics, include the standard ways to evaluate the data you gathered.

4. Write the Findings section, stating conclusions, and the Discussion section, which elaborates on the reasoning that led to the findings. The Discussion section should explain the relation between your actions, investigations and assessments of a situation, and your conclusions. It should also mention any further actions or research needed to make a decision or pursue the problem.

Writing recommendations: Depending on your report's purpose and format, write a separate list of recommendations based on your findings.

Checking the entire report: After drafting separate sections, unite them in one file and check for consistency in point of view, style, and logic. Edit the entire report to make sure it fits the reason you wrote it for specific readers.

Make changes that unite the perspective, tone, and style of each section. Use a grammar checker, for instance, to determine the average length of sentences and paragraphs. If one section uses many passive verbs and one uses active verbs, try to balance the two. Check for consistent uses of specialized terms and their spelling. Edit carefully so your report will be credible. (See chapter 4, "Editing Documents.")

10d Formatting a Report for Printing

Before you format a report for printing, look for examples of the type of report you wrote. Prepare models of sections, headers, and other details in reports you frequently write. Copy a sample report to your computer or a disk if you have it in an electronic file, or copy the formatting of particular sections into document files for storage.

10d–1 Model document files

Use templates for formatting your reports for printing. They help you arrange the sections of reports of any length or level of formality. If you consistently report to the same person or group, make a template that includes the preferences of those readers.

To make templates, use examples to determine the standard margins, preferred fonts and font sizes, and placement of page numbers. Consult examples about every detail of report formats, including their bindings and covers.

Preformatted macros can also include descriptive language and section introductions that are frequently repeated in reports submitted for similar purposes. For example, in a template file for, say, minutes of meetings, you can create and store a macro that contains the phrase "The meeting was called to order at. . . ." Then when you get to that point in your formatted meeting report, you can type the keystrokes you have assigned to the macro and the phrase will appear in your file. After you insert a macro, always reread the model language to check that its content and syntax fit your specific use.

10d–2 Sections and headings

Long, formal reports often have clearly separate sections because they have multiple audiences. Some readers may need to know your findings and recommendations immediately. Some may want to check the methods used to analyze data. Some may read only your review of the literature to identify other work about the topic or problem or review actions taken before the report was written. Readers want to locate these sections quickly.

Use a consistent outline, with sequential numbers and letters that separate sections and subsections. Depending on instructions and examples, you may want to apply different fonts, font sizes, and text styles at each level of heading. Headings for major sections might be printed in bold, with underline or italics for subheadings. Always use tabs to indent headings and the numbering systems that organize them (see 5e–1, "Indenting").

10d–3 Special parts of report documents

Instructions and models will help you decide whether to prepare the following special parts of reports, which require special attention.

Title page: A title page indicates a report's purpose, the dates of activities it concerns, and its intended readership. The title page often specifically names readers to whom the report is submitted and indicates the date of submission: "Submitted To: Parking Commission, Redwood City, January 23, 1997."

Summary: A one-page summary may be placed immediately after a title page. This is a concise statement of the report's findings and recommendations. Determine if your readers expect a summary. If your report will go to more than one readership, prepare an introductory summary for each group, tailored to their distinct use of it.

Abstract: An abstract of the report may be needed, especially if it is to be included in a database. The abstract should be an edited series of sen-

tences that summarize each section of the report, in the order in which the sections are presented (see 9e–2, "Abstracts and summaries"). Place the abstract on the first page of the report, below the title.

10e Using Graphics in Reports

Reports often use graphics to clarify and highlight written information. Pictures, charts, graphs, tables, icons, company logos, and other diagrams fulfill many functions. They present analyses of data, efficiently communicate results, and help readers remember your findings.

With word processing you can place graphics anywhere in your document, including pages that also contain text. But do not use graphics excessively. Too many diagrams, charts, and tables can distract from your statements or be confusing.

10e–1 Preliminary choices

To decide how much a report should rely on graphics, answer the following questions.

Will your word processing program insert already created graphics? Look in your screen menus and in your word processing manual for functions like Insert Picture, Import, and Graphics. Try out these functions before you need them at the last minute. If your school or company uses graphics for its stationery, get an electronic version to use in your documents. Store it in a separate file for repeated uses.

Can your word processing program create graphics? Word processing programs come equipped with built-in graphics programs. Consult screen help and a manual. Try out button bars, file menus, and lists of commands. Become familiar with the effects that various commands accomplish so you can make graphics yourself.

Does a report really need graphics to enhance its information? Do not use graphics if you cannot produce effective, professional effects with them or if they are not customary in the type of report you have written.

10e–2 Visual possibilities

The following possibilities will help you get started using graphics.

LISTS. For efficiency, list points and information. Indent lists from the left margin with tab stops, to ensure that they will print in even columns. Mark their items with sequential numbers (1, 2, 3), letters (A, B, C), or bullets (• • •). Many word processing programs have Number, Renumber, and Bullet features that insert marks and arrange lists.

Figure 10.1   Bar Graph in Student Paper

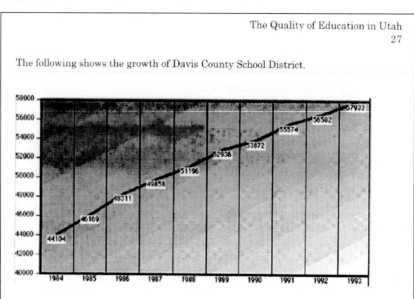

The Quality of Education in Utah
27

The following shows the growth of Davis County School District.

Growth in the State necessitates growth in education, especially in those school districts which are growing exceptionally fast. Otherwise the problems that do not seem so big now, will soon be unmanageable.[37]

The Legislature needs to reduce class sizes, buy more new textbooks and supplies, provide for the growth in the State, encourage parents to become more involved in education, encourage students to get further education after high school and provide alternatives for those who do not want to seek further education. All of

---

[37]This graph and information was obtained from the World Wide Web on August 10, 1995 at the following address: http://www.davis.k12.ut.us/growth.html.

CHARTS AND GRAPHS.   You can use charts and graphs to illustrate patterns of change and proportions. Charts may be composed of bars arranged horizontally or vertically, of segments of a circle (pie charts), or of plotted lines or points (scatter graphs that simultaneously show two variables, like change and volume). A Chart function can easily create various charts. Experiment with this function before you need to use it.

TABLE 10.1 HANDWRITING VS. WORD PROCESSING	
Handwriting	**Word Processing**
Slow	Fast
Variable according to person writing	Consistent appearance
Requires erasing	Allows deleting and rewording

TABLES. Tables organize information in columns and rows. Each cell (the intersection of a column and a row), can be sized to fit the data in it. Tables are not used only for numbers. They may organize written information to show contrasts, as in Table 10.1. This is a cell table, with a border around its column titles, which are shaded and larger than the items in the cells below them.

Word processing will also quickly format marginal comments on sections and paragraphs of a document. For instance, you might want to put a note next to a text paragraph like this. (See 7d–1, "Making notes from sources.")

Make a marginal note with the Table function.

DIAGRAMS AND PICTURES. You can draw pictures and diagrams with your computer and insert them in reports. Using a Picture or Draw function you can make curved and straight lines, circles, arrows, and other shapes. You

PRINTING A REPORT: A CHECKLIST

1. Use Outline View before printing to check for consistently formatted sequential headings. Check for consistent numbers and letters throughout the report.
2. Use Print Preview to check the entire report for consistent page margins, page numbers, headers, and footers.
3. Print a preliminary copy of parts of the report to check for formatting problems you may have missed while viewing the report on the screen. Are graphics placed correctly on pages?
4. Use the best available printer.
5. If you have included graphics that would benefit from color printing, check possibilities for printing in color (see chapter 6, "Printing Your Documents").
6. Use the best available paper.
7. As you print, check the pages of the report for even print quality and sequential page numbers.
8. Reports may be circulated among readers and then filed as official documents. Check instructions and examples to choose a suitably durable binding for the report.

can make a small diagram to insert in a frame and you can vary its size. Practice making pictures and diagrams before you decide to add them to a report so you can easily control their size and placement on pages.

The Next Time You Write

1. Find a report in a magazine, company publication, or other source. Use it to answer questions important for your own report writing: What elements show that it was written for a specific purpose and readership, including its title and submission information? What sections does it separate formally with headings? If this report does not indicate separate sections with headings, identify places in it where it refers to earlier sources, methods, and findings or recommendations. Do these sections follow the conventional order of sections? If not, what is the effect of a different order on your clarity about the information in the report?

2. Try out tables, borders, and any other visual effects your word processing program allows you to make yourself. Open a document you have written and experiment with the appearance of the text by using various graphic effects to highlight and clarify some of its points.

3. Note the kinds of reports you write, including very informal ones for yourself. Use those you have already written to make templates that follow their formats. Title these templates and save them in a special folder or directory.

11
Letters and Memos

This chapter describes how word processing can save you time in writing correspondence. It explains the conventional parts of formal letters and memos and how to arrange them. It discusses making models of conventional portions. It also shows how writing with a computer helps to achieve specific positive results in requests and applications.

11a Short Cuts for Writing Letters and Memos

Writing letters and memos with a computer helps you correspond more frequently because it not only increases the relative speed of writing and printing correspondence but makes it easier to format the many standard forms of both letters and memos.

11a–1 Use standard templates.

Your word processing program probably provides some standard templates that allow you to enter the language you usually use for parts of business correspondence, legal documents, and frequently sent memos. Check a manual for advice on how to use and modify standard templates. (Also see 5b, "Templates.")

11a–2 Make your own templates.

You can also create your own templates. For instance, you can create a file that contains the typical opening information, spacing, and closing information that you use in correspondence. (See 5b, "Templates," for more information about creating template files.)

11a–3 Merging data

Most word processing programs can combine files. You can, for instance, print letters and memos with addresses and greetings that vary from person to person but that contain the same content for the letter or memo itself. A Print Merge function will enable you to insert varying content into a model format. Merging correspondence with variable addresses obviously requires a standard message, so make sure your message can be sent to all your correspondents.

11b Letters

11b–1 Standard parts of a letter

The following standard parts appear in all but the most informal letters and notes, and even in many of them. When you write or format these components of letters, spell out names, the month, and greetings. Abbreviate the names of states (VA, UT), "Street" ("St.") and like words, and countries for letters sent outside the United States.

Your address: Your address may be printed on your letterhead, or you may enter it at the top of the page using a template. (See 11a, "Short Cuts for Writing Letters and Memos.")

Current date: Many word processing programs will insert the current date in a designated spot. Automatic dating functions usually change to the current date each time you reopen the document. Do not use this function if you will later need to know the date a letter was written.

Recipient's address: This is the inside (envelope) address. When you send a letter to a co-worker (but not a memo), place a generic term like "Campus" or "Company" after the co-worker's office address.

Greeting: Do not use first names ("Dear Joe") unless you know a recipient personally. You can place a handwritten first name over a printed one when you sign a letter. Do this if you know a business correspondent well but someone else prepared your letter with only a title and last name.

Do not assume that any group of recipients is entirely male. If you do not know a recipient, use a greeting that is neutral about gender and status, not "Dear Sir." Some alternatives: "Dear University of Texas–El Paso," "Dear Editor," "Dear Admissions Director," "Dear Dean of Humanities," "Dear Parking Administration."

Subject (optional): Some letters require a subject line above the greeting, as in "Subject: Your Vacation," two line spaces above "Dear Doctor Quinn." Check models of similar letters and an organization's practices.

Body: The content of a letter or memo should be pointed and brief unless you are writing a personal letter or preparing a request, an explanation of a legal problem, or a letter that will become an official document.

Closing: "Sincerely" is usual. Enter the word two line spaces below the body of the letter, above your signature.

Name: Your typed name, with a relevant title directly below it.

Initials (optional): In business correspondence, initials identify who wrote the letter, in capital letters; these are followed by the initials of the person who prepared the letter (if the signer did not), in lowercase letters. "KAK/sjm" might mean that Kenneth A. Keeper composed a letter prepared by Sam James Moot.

Enclosures (optional): Use "Encl." to indicate that you have enclosed something with the letter. "Encl." along with "under separate cover"

Figure 11.1   Formal Business Letter

2522 North 3rd Ave.
Chicago, IL 60614

May 2, 1996

TCS Marketing
Human Resources Department
1350 East Jamestown Ave.
Platteville, WI 53818

Dear Human Resources Department:

This letter is to inform you of my interest in TCS Marketing's Customer
Service Representative position.

I am very interested in the position, not only because I've heard won-
derful things about TCS Marketing, but because of my education and
training in marketing.

I would bring to TCS over three years of full-time experience in marketing, a B.A. in Business from the University of Illinois–Chicago, a positive attitude, and a willingness to learn. I am very dependable, a hard
worker, and a person who enjoys the feeling of a job well done.

Please find my résumé and list of references enclosed.

I look forward to speaking with you further about the position and my
qualifications. Please call me during the day at 708–456–2345 or in the
evening at 708–322–1543.

Thank you for considering my application.

Sincerely,

Robin Covington

---

would indicate that you simultaneously sent the recipient a package in addition to a letter.

   CC: or BCC (optional): Indicate any copies you send to others with
"CC:" followed by names. "BCC:" indicates "blind" copy; it tells the person
receiving the copy that the person to whom the letter is addressed does not

know that you sent this copy. It is only rarely appropriate to make this notation, such as when you have agreed to show a copy of a letter to a third party who is evaluating your correspondence.

Disk (optional): A disk notation indicates where you have stored the letter or memo on your computer: "Dsk: Agn:Sub" might indicate that the letter is stored in the "Submitted" subdirectory of the "Assignments" directory.

Headers (optional): Letters longer than one page need a header on subsequent pages for the recipient's name, the date, and the page number. Print pages after the first page on plain paper, not letterhead stationery.

11b–2 Formal and informal letters

FORMAL LETTERS. Conventional practices determine how to space business and other formal letters on the page. Usually, arrange the parts of letters by centering your return address or using right alignment for it. Use left alignment for the date. Use left alignment for your recipient's address and all other sections of the letter. In traditional formatting, indent the first line of each paragraph in the body of the letter. You can also use full justification for some business correspondence. (See 5f–2, "Alignment.")

Organizations and the departments within them select a distinct appearance for their correspondence. They use specified fonts, font sizes, page margins, greetings and salutations, and styles for the arrangement of the letter's parts. They may frequently use standard language for parts of letters that have legal implications. Do not vary these customs when you write on behalf of an organization.

INFORMAL LETTERS. Even the most casual letters to family and friends should include the date and an address where you can receive a response. Format informal correspondence so it is easy to read.

11c Memos: Purposes and Format

Memos communicate within groups and among co-workers. They may give instructions, make announcements, transmit other documents, define and justify policy and actions, or respond to any of these purposes. Organizations may have printed stationery for memos that includes standard parts as vertically listed headings:

Date:
To:
From:
Subject:

Memos are usually brief, but they may also be lengthy reports of activities or project results (see chapter 10, "Reports"). Like letters, longer memos should include headers at the top of every page after the first page; the header gives the memo's recipients, the subject, and the page number. Always format memos with the standard form used by your organization. In general, do not vary the font, font size, page margins, or informative lines that are expected by your group.

Figure 11.2   Business Memo

To:	TCS Hiring Committee
From:	Nancy Smith, Human Resources Manager
Date:	May 10, 1996
Subject:	Robin Covington Interview

Please mark your calendars for an interview at 11 a.m. on Wednesday, May 29. Robin Covington from Chicago will be here to interview for the Customer Service Representative position. After a tour of TCS, we'll meet in the conference room for the interview.

Please bring to the interview a copy of Robin's résumé plus questions from each of your departments that will help us determine her qualifications.

Thanks for your help.

11d Writing Successful Requests and Application Letters

Word processing can help you write specialized letters and memos that make requests of your correspondents. Use the following guidelines to help you prepare letters and memos to persuade readers to consider your requests.

11d–1 Use formats and language familiar to readers.

Readers are most likely to respond positively if you establish their trust by acknowledging their customs. If you can, locate examples of letters and other materials written by your correspondents. Read examples carefully to get a sense of their modes of expression, frequently used terms, and formatting styles. Always format an application letter or request as closely as possible to your recipient's formats to make your letter appear familiar.

If you cannot locate examples written by your correspondent, read examples like those your recipient customarily reads. Documents written in the recipient's field of interest, for similar purposes, and among people your recipient knows all provide a context for your writing.

→ *SECRETS OF SUCCESSFUL WRITERS* ←
Request and Application Letters

- Do not use e-mail for important requests or applications. E-mail is informal and does not always reach its intended recipients.

11d–2 Edit, check, recheck, and get help.

Obviously, letters of application and requests should be as carefully written, edited, and printed as you can make them. Talk to trustworthy advisers about your purpose for writing. Try out ideas and discuss details of content and form. Follow the guidelines in chapters 5, "Formatting Documents," and 6, "Printing Your Documents," for editing, checking, rechecking, and printing documents. Ask a reliable editor to comment on a printed draft. Make suggested changes and corrections and ask for a quick review before printing a final copy. Finally, always finish in time to deliver the document to the right person on time.

Do not use e-mail for important requests or applications. E-mail is informal and does not always reach its intended recipients. It will not make the impact of a printed document.

11d–3 Take time for careful control of your content.

Word processing can give you time to think about details of your actual situation and purpose when you write requests and applications. Focus on the actual writing situation, not on tangential issues.

For instance, if you apply for a job, be sure your application demonstrates that you want the advertised position and can do it, not that you need *any* position. If you apply for admission to a program, or for a scholarship or a grant, be sure to emphasize your desire to pursue the outcome of the program to which you apply. Professional schools, for instance, offer professional training, so an application to a law school should show that you want to become an attorney, not that you want to go into politics. If you are writing a request for payment, for special treatment by a company, or for an exception to a policy, focus on reasons for your request, not on general circumstances. Do not imply rejection of your correspondent or of policies that you want changed.

The Next Time You Write

1. While you are not under pressure to find a job or gain admission to a program, draft a letter of application that demonstrates your qualifications and fit to a position or situation. Show this draft to a friend who has a job

or position like the one you are writing about. Ask for comments on your letter's appearance and content.

2. Examine some of the impersonal mail you receive during one week to determine how business correspondence is written to appear simultaneously personal and suitable for a large audience. How do you react to such letters? Are they persuasive? What features direct these letters to you individually?

12
Résumés

This chapter explains the advantages of using word processing to prepare résumés. It explains how to arrange the parts of a résumé, keep it updated, make multiple versions for applications to various positions, and ensure its formal appearance.

A résumé, which in academic communities is called a *vita* (or *curriculum vitae*), is the organized list of the credentials and work experience of a job applicant. Résumés require attention to a number of details whose conventions differ in various work and study communities.

You can purchase commercial software programs that help create résumés for specialized purposes. But in any word processing program you can list and rearrange the items of a résumé to fit the requirements of particular positions. Word processing helps ensure the exactness of items you include and improves their appearance on the page.

12a Résumés as Ongoing Compositions

A résumé is a continuing composition (see chapter 7, "Ongoing Compositions: Records and Notes"). You write it over time, keeping it up to date by adding new items and deleting others as your experience and credentials grow and your interests and achievements change. Use the following guidelines to produce this ongoing writing.

1. Create a master résumé file. Keep it in an accessible folder or directory, so you remember to add new items and categories to it. Each time you learn a new skill, have a new work or educational experience, travel extensively, change jobs, or experience major personal changes that are relevant to education and employment, add these items to this document.

2. Rearrange the items in new categories as your experience grows. Categories for skills, work experiences, and achievements may need reorganization. If you take on new duties at a job, for instance, you may want to create a new heading that identifies this kind of assignment. You can put in this category previous experiences that are relevant to the new category. You may also want to eliminate old categories.

12b Arranging Information in a Résumé

Begin your résumé with standard information: your name, street address, telephone and fax numbers, and e-mail and Web page addresses if you have them (see chapter 18, "Connecting with Other Writers," and chapter 21, "Writing for the World Wide Web").

12c

Next, specify your educational background: schools attended, academic majors and minors, and certificates and degrees and their dates, with the names of institutions where you earned them.

A résumé also includes other notable information about your schooling and early jobs, later work experience, honors, job changes, and career training and development. It presents this information in two sequences. The following suggestions will help you organize information.

1. First list any activities relevant to your current application that you undertook before your first job, in chronological order, from youth to your most recent graduation.

2. Next list work experiences and changes in reverse chronological order, from the most recent to older items.

3. Use reverse chronology within each category of the résumé that describes your experience, whether it emphasizes your skills, highlights the kinds of positions you have held, or lists the progression of your education and achievements.

4. When you make a new version of your résumé for new applications, rearrange the order of categories to highlight particular qualifications. Use word processing to rearrange blocks of information and to insert relevant items without retyping the entire document.

12c Formatting Different Versions for Different Job Applications

Each time you apply for a position, you need a new version of your résumé. After you complete a master résumé file, make one or more copies to rearrange for different kinds of jobs. (Always copy the master document before revising it. Do not make formatting changes on the master, only carefully typed additions.)

For instance, if you want a construction job in the summer and an office job in the fall, use two different copies of your master résumé with the items rearranged for each kind of work. Emphasize evidence of physical strength (regular weightlifting? river-rafting vacation?) on the summer résumé, and highlight filing, word processing, and work-study experience on the fall one. State objectives and personal goals relevant to the job you are applying for.

12c–1 Follow models.

If it is possible without invading a worker's privacy, read the résumés of job applicants who successfully applied for jobs similar to the one you want, perhaps those of your friends. Use formatting details in those examples as a guide. The appearance of successful résumés varies from one community to another. Special characters and attention-getting formats may be exactly right—or entirely wrong—for a particular employer or position. Use the many available guides for writing résumés to determine appropriate forms.

12c–2 Use consistent spacing.

Any résumé requires consistent indentations and spacing within and between items. Use single spacing in the items of your résumé, and double-space between them. Always use tab stops, not the space bar, to evenly indent categories and items within them.

12c–3 Always edit and reedit added items.

Each time you add an item to a résumé or rearrange its categories, edit it again to check headings, the indentation of its items, and other details, especially spelling. Résumés contain many proper names and titles, so spell-checking will suggest incorrect alternatives. Misspelling is one of the worst errors that can appear in a résumé. Reread for correctness more than once.

12d Printing a Résumé

Apply a printing checklist each time you print a résumé (see "A Last-Minute Checklist" in chapter 6, page 53). Use Print Preview to check headings and consistent page margins. Use the best available paper.

Consistency in print quality and in the arrangement of items on each page of a résumé is your readers' first view of your attention to detail and organization. Take time to ensure that items are placed correctly on each page.

> **SECRETS OF SUCCESSFUL WRITERS**
> *Good First Impressions*

- Use position descriptions to guide your formatting so that prospective employers can easily notice your relevant qualifications.
- Each time you add or rearrange items, edit the résumé again. Check headings, indentations, and especially spelling. Misspelling is one of the worst errors that can appear in a résumé.
- Remember: Your résumé is used by prospective employers to eliminate applicants. It must match the job description, be easy to follow, and demonstrate your work habits.

Figure 12.1   Sample Résumé

ROBIN COVINGTON

2522 North 3rd Ave.	708–322–1543 home
Chicago, IL 60614	708–456–2345 office
http://www.aol.com/~robin12/	robin12@aol.com

EDUCATION

B.A., Business
   University of Illinois–Chicago, April 1996

EXPERIENCE

University of Illinois–Chicago, Business Computer Lab
   Training Supervisor, May 1994–Present.
      Hire, schedule, train, and supervise 12 part-time computer consultants. Provide technical support for students, staff, and faculty on industry-standard software programs and Internet programs for both PC and Macintosh operating systems. (Full-time, 30+ hours a week.)

University of Illinois–Chicago, Admissions Office
   Admissions Clerk, September 1992–May 1994.
      Processed applications; filed, sorted, and mailed correspondence to students; answered questions concerning admissions to the University of Illinois. (Full-time, 30+ hours a week.)

SSI Software, Inc.
   Research Coordinator, January 1991–September 1992.
      Invoiced clients, ran reports, processed mail and phone orders. Worked with representatives from various software companies. (Part-time, 10+ hours a week.)

SKILLS

Customer Service	Technical Writing
• Order Processing	• Procedures
• Report Writing	• HTML (Web Pages)
Spreadsheet and Database	Word Processing
• Excel	• WordPerfect
• FileMaker Pro	• MS Word

ASSOCIATIONS

Future Marketing Representatives of America, American Society for Training and Development.

The Next Time You Write

1. Take time to begin a master résumé before you are under pressure to apply for a job. Ask a friend with a job for a copy of a successful application letter and résumé, and show the friend your drafted résumé for comments.

2. If you have a résumé in a word processing file now, print a copy and check that it is current and follows the details of arrangement and editing noted in this chapter. Make corrections. Spell-check the corrected file, noticing how often words appear that your spell checker does not recognize. Check the spelling of names and titles yourself and correct any errors.

3. Duplicate your current résumé file and edit the copy to accompany an application for a job in a different field or one with different requirements than your current position. Add the new items you will recall as you imagine a change. Edit the new résumé, print a copy, and show it to someone in the new field for comments.

13
Taking Examinations

> Some short-answer standardized tests and written examinations are now administered on computers. This chapter suggests how to prepare for these testing situations and lists ways to use the computer effectively in them.

Prepare carefully for taking any kind of examination with a computer. You need information about how the test will be conducted and practice to be as comfortable as possible. The following guidelines will help.

13a Guidelines for Using a Computer to Answer Questions

1. Do not automatically use a computer. Taking a standardized examination with a computer may be an option but not a requirement. If so, consider how the computer version of the test may affect your score. If you have a choice, avoid using a computer unless you have experience with one in this testing situation. (Some experts think that taking noncomputerized versions of tests produces higher scores.) In either case, read all the information about the test carefully and as early as possible.

2. Get to know unfamiliar computers. If the operating system to be used differs from the one you are familiar with (for example, it is a Mac and you use a PC), spend time practicing on the unfamiliar system. If you will be using a mouse, arrows, or other key commands for the first time, practice the new method. School and library computer labs may have computers you can try out.

3. Before you begin the test itself, explore the computer. Get used to its keyboard. Find and use the mouse and practice moving the insertion point or cursor. Be as comfortable with the computer as time permits before taking the test.

4. Get the instructions for operating the testing program as early as you can and read them carefully. They may include information about specific ways to use the computer during the test.

5. Use any available practice software to prepare. It may allow you to answer practice questions formatted like those on the test itself. Practice as much as you can with the testing software.

6. Do not let a computer hurry you. Standardized tests are usually timed, so answering questions with a computer may make you feel rushed because you must follow technical directions exactly as you choose answers. But focus on and verify each answer to check both its accuracy and its placement in the right space.

Figure 13.1 Princeton Review's GRE Practice Test

```
00:31                          Section 1                          1 of 38

        The Ottomans, who developed bureaucratic systems of governing long before the ancient
        Romans, were also indefatigable about keeping official documentation, and as a result of this,
        are noted for having the world's most extensive ------ of civil proceedings.


                                    ○  denouncement

                                    ○  chronicle

                                    ○  duration

                                    ○  hypothesis

                                    ○  mastery



  TEST   SECTION    REVIEW   MARK                                        ?      PREV   NEXT
```

13b Guidelines for Using a Computer to Write Essay Tests

If a testing situation permits, you may want to write essay examinations with a computer if you usually use word processing to write. But avoid word processing for writing an exam if you are a very slow typist or are new to word processing.

Before the exam, review the guidelines for using word processing to write essays and other assigned writing (see chapter 8, "Essays and Other Assigned Writing"). Plan how you will compose answers in a limited time. Planning and pacing your writing are crucial. The following guidelines will help you write more easily.

1. Get to know an unfamiliar computer before you must use it. Use its keyboard, operating system, mouse, function keys, menus, ribbon, and ruler bars. Practice moving the insertion point, selecting and moving text, deleting text, and scrolling through screens. Practice using the computer's Undo command. If the computer uses unfamiliar writing software, be sure to practice with it. Become as comfortable with the computer as time permits.

2. Ask beforehand about the number, kind, and weight of the questions to be asked. Learn as much as possible about how to allocate your time dur-

ing the test. Ask specific questions to help you plan for parts of the examination and finish in time to review and edit your answers. Write with a watch or clock in view.

3. Practice typing answers to questions under time pressure. Use earlier questions from similar tests or create practice questions about the subject of the test. As you practice, push yourself to type and revise as quickly as you can. Consider the results. Practice again.

4. Divide your writing time into portions for each question. Obviously, allot the most time to heavily weighted questions. An examination may set an absolute time limit for each question. But plan to give as much time as you can to questions that first appear difficult and less time to those you immediately know how to approach.

5. Type each question into the answer file as you begin answering it. Take time to copy questions, or the important parts of long ones, so you read them carefully as you begin to write answers. You can select and move parts of copied questions into your answer.

6. Break the copied questions into meaningful parts, if possible. Under each, list points to make and examples to include. Taking time to outline your first thoughts below the question will speed writing the entire response. You can type answers between items on your list. If you do not have time to finish an answer later, these notes in outline form will indicate the direction you planned to follow.

7. Answer questions directly. Follow cues in the question to organize the answer. Examiners want direct, clearly organized answers. Use the questions you copy to sequence your points and to suggest language for answers.

Most questions imply a way to answer, so use them to organize points in the terms the question sets. For instance, "compare," "contrast," "classify," "describe the process of," "analyze" ("examine the parts of") or "combine" ("synthesize") are cues that will help you arrange and develop answers.

Use the vocabulary and specialized terms common in the field in which the question is asked. Write directly. Avoid too formal and too casual language.

8. Reread your answers quickly to make obvious corrections and insert brief additional support for your points. You must finish an examination in the time allotted, so do not count on time for editing, but quickly review each answer to improve it.

Correct obvious errors and delete stray comments that may confuse the examiner. Look for accidentally added or omitted or deleted words and phrases; insert question marks in parentheses or brackets where you are unsure of a date or the spelling of a name; elaborate with relevant names, references, and other details in parentheses where they support your points. If you have time to spell-check, do so, but be cautious about accepting suggestions.

The Next Time You Write

1. When you know you must take a standardized test, check immediately to find out if it is administered with a computer. Search for practice software and work with it as much as time permits. Decide whether taking the written version would be best for you. You usually cannot return to already-answered questions on computerized tests, but your score may be available immediately after the test.

2. Try writing any composition as quickly as you can, and then reread it to judge the kind of omissions, accidental deletions, and errors you habitually make when you type quickly. Practice until your pace is both quick and relatively accurate.

14
Writing and Reading Creative Texts

14a

This chapter points out how word processing can help you write and read creative pieces by applying individual processes to fit your personal goals. It shows how to use word processing to help with writing fiction, plays, and poetry and with managing files. It also suggests how to use word processing to help you imitate notable texts and analyze their language.

No one can tell a writer what to say in poetry, fiction, drama, or experimental forms of writing. But word processing helps you write these forms in multiple ways. It helps you keep track of your development by storing dated versions of your writing. Its flexibility also encourages experimentation as you search for and rearrange patterns in your writing and in models you want to understand from a writer's perspective. It helps you make experimental substitutions and deletions and try out arrangements of words, lines, and segments of text. It can also help you pay more attention to sound and visual patterns by allowing you to see them in special formats.

You can store creative files and later find selected segments of them, as you can with any kind of writing. But word processing programs will also number lines of prose and poetry, apply varied paragraph styles to sections, and allow you to include visual effects in written language. It helps you develop individual pieces and experiment with their style and form.

14a Keeping Track of Ideas

Manage creative writing as carefully as you do assignments and professional work. List the file names of your documents in an ongoing, dated log, with notes about the content, form, and special qualities of each piece of writing. (See 7b, "Managing Record Files," and 7e, "Research Logs and Storage.") Use separate folders or directories for keeping your own ongoing writing, your work from earlier time periods, and notes you may want to use in new pieces. For instance, you can open a note file of background information to consult and copy while you write fiction. (See 2a–2, "Make notes," and 7d, "Notes from Sources.") Story ideas, plot outlines, character sketches, and bits of description or dialogue can be copied or kept open to remind you of images, lines of action, or details about a character's biography. If a piece of writing will detail a setting and the movements of characters, you can copy a map from a library's database to consult as you describe the territory.

14b Creative Composing

Creative writing is usually an ongoing composition (see chapter 7, "Ongoing Compositions: Records and Notes"). Try out functions that help you experiment as you develop ideas. Obviously, the nonstop writing encouraged by word processing helps you discover and elaborate your ideas. It allows you to add new material to stored files, divide longer pieces into new ones for expansion, and search through files for language and ideas you want to use. You can make notes in unique voices indicated by font styles and special characters and insert them with drawings and diagrams that show movements within a composition. You can play with the language in a thesaurus, substituting words in your poetry and writing from the sounds and images they suggest.

Use a computer's full range of font, margin, and spacing options to highlight and emphasize the possible visual designs of written language. For instance, some fonts allow you to write in codes and arrange the "letters" to make diagrams. Concrete poetry plays with the visual formatting of words and letters, sometimes placing words in patterns that fit their meaning. Syllabic poetry is controlled by counted syllables in its lines, so you might want to use a hyphenation function to view words in their possible segments. You can also make a table in which one cell represents one syllable, and each row represents a line. You can count lines or words in any highlighted section of your text to arrange them in patterns.

14c Practice and Imitation

Experiment with traditional and unusual patterns of language that appear in all kinds of writing. The following suggestions will get you started.

14c–1 Model formats for plots

Make templates to use when you write special elements of creative texts. You can format indented and justified lines for poetry, change marks for dialogue among characters, and outline the acts and scenes of plays. Make standard outlines for stories and chapters of novels. For instance, "formula fiction" is often written with standard outlines for action and types of characters.

The complicated plot of a novel or drama and the qualities and actions of characters might also unfold in the columns of a table as you add cells and rearrange them over time. Such charts can be expanded with inserted character sketches, dialogue, and images, for later transfer to other work.

14c–2 Poetry

For poets, word processing can guide practice writing, for instance of traditional stanza forms such as sonnets, ballads, and rhymed couplets. Use templates to show the required number of syllables in each line of a standard stanza, the location of stressed and unstressed syllables within it, and its rhyme pattern at the ends of lines. Copy examples into these files to practice imitating their lines and filling in outlines you make with them.

14c–3 Stylistic imitation

Make templates with sentence patterns for stylistic practice. Gather examples of traditional figures of speech and create master files to practice their patterns. For instance, a simile form is "as (<u>soft</u>) as a (<u>cloud</u>)"; parallelism might follow "to (<u>see</u>) it is to (<u>want</u>) it." You can practice controlling your style with figures that coordinate and subordinate ideas or that require sequences of parallel forms. Copy striking examples to these files to imitate their uses of metaphors, similes, allusions, and sound patterns—rhyme, alliteration, assonance. Be sure to record the sources of examples.

14c–4 Imitating sentence patterns

To control your own writing, imitate the grammatical and syntactic elements in model sentences. Copy into your practice file sentences whose patterns catch your attention. Write new sentences that imitate these patterns or rearrange some of your own sentences imported from your logs. Visual representations of striking sentences help you craft your own, a process that will improve your ongoing composing.

14d Analyzing Reading

You can copy many examples of literature and important documents from the Internet and library databases. When you open electronic texts in your word processing program, they are as available for analysis and experimentation as your own writing. You can read and analyze the paragraphs, sentences, and lines of Shakespeare's sonnets and plays, the speeches of Martin Luther King Jr., the Declaration of Independence, and many other exemplary pieces.

To understand how notable language achieves its results, apply word processing tools. For instance, sentence-by-sentence analysis with a grammar checker will show how the sequence of the grammatical elements of sentences—subjects, verbs, objects—helps to control the reader's emotions and understanding. Try substitute arrangements to see how they change your response to ideas in a piece.

Temporarily substitute variant words from your thesaurus for selected language, to gauge the impact of the author's diction. Use word processing features to temporarily segment, rearrange, delete, and add language to the text, again to assess the effects of the original choices.

→ **SECRETS OF SUCCESSFUL WRITERS** ←
If You Want to Publish

- Always read issues of publications to which you want to submit creative writing. Editors respond negatively when it is clear that your submission does not fit the range of form and content they favor and publish.

If you want to improve your understanding of how the language of an example controls its effects, add new passages in the style of the author and print the whole piece. Ask for responses from someone who has read the original.

When you are analyzing a document you have copied, use these and other functions to prepare evidence for points about the relation of the document's language to its theme and images.

The Next Time You Write

1. Use a creative text you have written or a copied example to make a template for others you will write later.

2. Copy a piece of writing you admire and want to imitate. Use word processing to analyze its sentences and then write new ones that imitate their language, patterns, and figures of speech.

3. Practice translating copied poetry to prose, and the reverse. Break lines and change paragraph styles to highlight effects in your new versions.

4. Format a model file for a poem with a predetermined rhyme scheme, number of syllables per line, and number of lines per stanza. Then choose a word that evokes an image for you and write statements in this model from your response to it. Revise to improve by changing the identity of the imagined speaker in the poem at the middle of each stanza.

15
Personal and Professional Publishing

This chapter describes ways of preparing your writing for distribution on your own and through a professional printer. It discusses using simple design techniques of desktop publishing for documents you distribute yourself. It addresses matters to consider when preparing electronic versions of manuscripts for professional publishers.

Publishing is making your writing available to a readership. It can mean distributing a well-designed document to a group you know or having professionals distribute it. Desktop publishing programs, used by professionals to design texts, can help you create attractive documents for personal distribution. Computers also make it possible to prepare electronic copies of manuscripts on diskettes for professional publishing.

15a Word Processing and Desktop Publishing

Word processing programs work with words, so their main function is making it easier to write and edit. They will create documents with tables, graphs, charts, inserted pictures, and many types of headers. They will align text and graphics, position them horizontally on pages, insert borders and frames, and do many of the tasks needed to make visually attractive texts.

When your writing depends on careful or elaborate design to achieve its results, you may want to use a desktop publishing program. Obviously, without experience and some training as a designer, you will not produce professional work. But desktop publishing programs make it easier to assemble and arrange words, pictures, and graphics from many sources, with extra control of their spacing, fonts, colors, size, location on pages, and other details. These tools are fun to explore and indispensable for doing professional page design.

Testing a desktop publishing program in a sample task will encourage you to look at all written documents *as* documents. The visual design of pages influences readers. After you try a desktop publishing program, you may want to use it when presentation is crucial in school and work situations. Many copy services, schools, and businesses have desktop publishing facilities you can use when you want a special effect.

Trying out desktop publishing will also alert you to look for readily available features of word processing that accomplish similar results. Explore similar features in word processing on a practice file, to see how you might improve the look of your work.

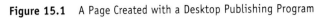

Figure 15.1   A Page Created with a Desktop Publishing Program

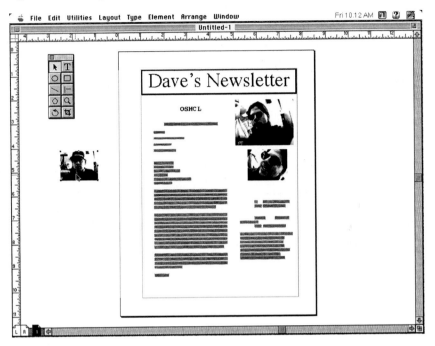

15b From Disk to Book and Article

Many publishers request not only manuscript pages of your writing, but a disk with an electronic version of the document. Submission in electronic form can reduce the time between writing and publication.

To make a useful disk containing your document, you will need to know the publisher's preferred format. The publisher will specify Mac, DOS, or Windows formatting and other details. For instance, you may need to merge separate sections and chapters in one document that has continuous pagination and consistent formats, with the same spacing of headers and footers on every page. You may need to make a table of contents for an entire document and place footnotes at the bottom of pages, after chapters, or at the end of the document (see 9e, "Writing Specialized Parts of Research Documents"). You can also create indexes—paginated lists of words and phrases you identify in a text.

Many publishers want stripped-down text files, without any formatting, so they can transfer your text to template files. They take responsibility for the major elements of visual design of submitted manuscripts and disks.

The Next Time You Write

1. Choose a document you have edited and printed to plan the visual effects you would want to add to it for personal publication to a large group. List these effects and then determine whether your word processing program could apply them by experimenting and looking in its manual for possibilities.

2. Finish a document by experimenting with a desktop publishing program applied to a copy of the document. Then practice using features in your word processing program that help you achieve similar effects.

3. Use desktop publishing for homemade cards, stationery, or other printed items you frequently use. If you like the results, print them on special papers for regular use. Try making envelopes for cards, using the Create Envelope feature.

4. The next time you read a magazine or journal, notice the formatting applied to its articles. What features of your word processing program could you use to achieve similar effects?

ART THREE

One Writer, Many Computers

16

Using Computer Networks

This chapter describes different types of computer networks, network accounts, guidelines for network security, and access to the Internet. It tells how you can obtain a network account and create passwords. It also answers common questions about the Internet and lists time savers.

16a Understanding Networks

Computer networks are groups of connected computers. Both smaller groups (called Local Area Networks, or LANs) and larger ones (called Wide Area Networks, or WANs) can connect to even larger networks like the Internet. The Internet is the largest network in the world. It connects millions of computers and thousands of networks all over the world. Many people think that *network* and *Internet* are interchangeable terms, but people who have access to a network do not always have access to the Internet. (When we use the term *network*, we mean a non-Internet network such as you will find at your school, business, or library.)

System administrators (system operators) set up and operate computer networks. If your computer is connected to a network, you can connect to a computer called a "file server" or "server"—the computer that controls your organization's network. Once your computer is connected, you can use the network's software programs, access its files, send and receive electronic communications, and use its other resources. Computer networks, like telephone connections, allow computers to call, answer, and talk to each other.

16a–1 Network accounts

Sometimes you can use computers at work or school without having an account on a particular network. Libraries, for example, permit direct access to their network of online catalogs and databases without requiring users to have an account (see 9b, "Specialized Computer Databases and Electronic Sources"). In other situations, however, you must obtain an account on a network before being able to use it.

When you obtain a network account, you receive an account name and a password. An account name (also called a "login name," "user name," or "user ID") may contain your name, a nickname, or numbers. A standard procedure of many organizations is to assign account names that include your first initial plus all or seven letters of your last name. For example, Tim Allen may be given the account name "tallen." Other examples of account names might be the following:

rcg4235 (Ricky C. Glaser, phone extension 4235)
mduke (Mary Duke)
binge (Scott Hunt's nickname)
ariel (Ariel Holly)

Many organizations create accounts on their networks so that users can dial in to them from home using a computer and a modem.

16a-2 Passwords and security

To access a computer account, you must enter your account name and then your password. Passwords protect your account from others. Sometimes people try to break into computer networks to vandalize and steal information, so do not create a password that is a word that appears in the dictionary or includes your name. If your network permits, create a password that contains combinations of special characters, uppercase letters, and numbers. Make your password easy to remember. Some examples:

born2bwild
UT@2002
U2andUB40
Porsche911
4uMYdear

Your system administrators will advise you further about creating your password.

Warning: Do not give your password to *anyone*. If those who are in charge of your network (or claim to be in charge of your network) ask you for your password, do not give it to them. Protect your password the same way you protect the PIN number associated with your banking and credit card accounts.

16a-3 Internet access

Many universities, companies, and other organizations have networks that allow access to the Internet. But even if you have an account on a network or have obtained Internet software programs, you still may be unable to access the Internet. If so, you have two options for connecting.

COMMERCIAL ONLINE SERVICES. America Online, CompuServe, Delphi, Prodigy, and other commercial online services give customers accounts on their networks. Online services have specialized resources and services on their networks that are not always available to those on the Internet, like discussions, promotions, and sales services for their members only. But most online services also offer access to the Internet. Payment plans vary,

Figure 16.1   America Online Main Menu

but there are usually monthly fees plus extra charges for additional services and additional time above a specified minimum. Commercial online services can be a good place to begin accessing network resources and the Internet. They usually provide easy-to-install software, customer support, and free trial periods for prospective customers.

INTERNET ACCESS PROVIDERS.   Internet access providers usually offer fewer customer support and specialized resources than commercial services do. They may charge lower monthly fees, but configuring your computer to use an Internet access provider is usually more difficult than connecting to a commercial online service. However, Internet access providers often offer you more flexibility in the types of Internet software programs you can use and the variety of Internet resources you can access.

16b Understanding the Internet

Services and resources available on the Internet are expanding each day, so both experienced users and new users can find it difficult to keep up with what appears to be chaotic information about the Internet. But the Internet's functions can be described simply, as a list of actions that will help you understand the purpose of new resources.

Figure 16.2 Internet Access Provider Main Menu

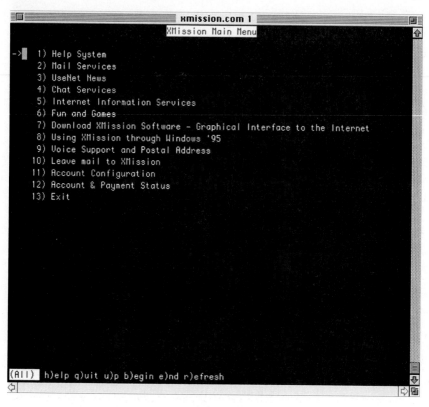

16b–1 What computers on the Internet can do

The Internet can help you write, conduct research, and communicate with others in four general ways.

CONNECT. The function that defines networks and the Internet is the ability to connect computers to each other. If you have access to the Internet, your computer can connect to various Internet "sites"—other computers connected to the Internet.

TRANSFER. When your computer is connected to the Internet, you can send and receive information to and from other computers. You can copy pictures, transfer word processing files and software programs, and send and receive other computer files.

SEARCH. Networked computers make available so many files that it helps to have a way to sort and search them easily. Search programs (see chapter 17, "Using the Internet for Research") can find various Internet sites that may have information you need, locating them by name of site, topic, and other data.

DISPLAY. Computers connected to the Internet can display electronic publications, including formatted texts, pictures, and multimedia sound and video clips. You can distribute similar content to other Internet users.

16b-2 What people on the Internet can do

Computers on the Internet can connect, transfer, search, and display information, so you can use them for many purposes. Here are four ways people use the Internet.

COMMUNICATE. You can communicate with friends, classmates, co-workers, and individuals or groups from around the world. E-mail and other communication programs provide quick and regular ways to correspond with others. Some programs enable real-time written conversations ("chats") in which you and others who have signed on to the same site can instantly see what each person is writing. Newer technologies allow video conferencing over the Internet.

LEARN. The Internet is like a large library of information, so connecting to it is a commitment to self-education. You can learn almost anything, from a biology course taught by a university to how to play the latest Garth Brooks song on the guitar. But the Internet is more than an archive of lessons and guitar chords. Sharing information is the foundation of communities on the Internet, so their members are usually eager to share what they learn with others. Individual users can participate in group discussions about short stories, TV sitcoms, current world events, and almost any other topic.

PLAY. Many locations on the Internet are devoted to entertaining, imaginative fun. You can find creative writers, science fiction buffs, or enthusiasts with many other imaginative interests. Entertainment sites allow you to copy software games, join in conversations about movies, and play fantasy role-playing games with people from around the world.

WRITE. The Internet is primarily a textual community based on the exchange of writing. When communicating, learning, and playing, you will be writing. Since reading and writing will occupy most of your time on the Internet, you can enjoy and invent many new ways to vary both activities. New ways of writing on the Internet, where the point is speedy response and tightly focused statements, encourage informal writing with little attention to editing. But the Internet can also be a place where well-crafted, highly polished documents can be published. Some traditional publishers even use the Internet to distribute electronic versions of printed publications (called "electronic magazines," or "e-zines").

16b-3 Common questions

The speed of your computer, the speed of your modem or network, the speed of computers you are connecting to, the number of other Internet users trying to connect to the same Internet site, and other variables all mean that you will sometimes encounter problems using the Internet. Be patient. Keep trying. Ask for help when necessary. The following are some common questions and answers.

"WHY CAN'T I CONNECT?"   A number of problems prevent connecting to an Internet site. When you dial in to your network account, computer phone lines may be busy. You may have mistyped your account name and password. Many systems are case-sensitive, meaning that you must use upper- or lowercase letters accurately in entering your name and password.

The Internet site you are trying to reach may have too many other computers connected to it. Popular Internet sites, where hundreds of thousands of connections are being made each day, are sometimes especially difficult to reach. Sometimes system administrators take Internet sites "off line" for upgrades and maintenance.

"WHERE DID THOSE FILES GO?"   When you cannot find a file you have copied from the Internet, you can check the directory that contains the Internet program you were using. Sometimes files are copied to directories called "Download" or "Attachment folder." Check the configuration (sometimes called "Preferences" or "Setup") of the program you are using to see if there is an option that will allow you to choose where to place files that you copy.

"WHY ARE MY FILES SCRAMBLED?"   When you open files you copy from the Internet, they are sometimes unreadable. Often files are "compressed" or "coded" to take up less space on the Internet and make transfer quicker. When this has happened, files must be "uncompressed" or "decoded" before using them. Decompression and decoding software is available on the Internet. (See 17c, "Retrieving Information from the Internet.")

Figure 16.3   Scrambled/Encoded File

```
M9&KXE&U&A1J/$N>!/5[\/9&9B\-3&48>3TYCZ1Y+3CLU34:OIU=F7$$C]B-(
M&^U_^7/YT@?EI(!GR4F_(/K2?Q_CSQGJ=P@R%&#B3E>G)<'NN"FL*1Z'N#YB
M^*25PLRI'78Y6HQN-B*:U8^?NXL[!N>P<((])UN43#_5J>&!#J&O7\?M:B5-
MJ";Z:G/38?NS';';':'X:A^A\NK=5J:O11JL]&^W^DK(^1-O\L9/7PURHF__ )+4
M4;?_ &:S_P#MQQ_Z.LID:3E>C \Q:G,W_P_P**A5U#RZ'R' HM5H+XVNV_+SZ_VWXWX^3C_Ov23' 't\_t;
M^5KK^D=::TH;K,P)(OOH5?\ [R3^OK)CYUS'&MU554M(M=#H=H@^?==2,8TX=
M</,,JSN'U69,C+%&%,?D/4N*%X\[ 94MQ1|:22HDI)))))))))^>"!7#+)^W_DGOAUL
M**:S?_P &+'28' 7'AX[\%W_CM,Fl0_\ E\;[5K56?2P\A**]+=-D@@_ULOF_C
M^^_;;;;;XX;
```

"How Do I Get Back to Where I Started?" When you begin using the Internet, you may find your computer connected to unfamiliar sites without knowing how you got there. Some Internet programs have buttons or menu options that will take you back to where you started. Other programs require pressing keys (like the Alt key and x) or typing "exit" to disconnect from a connection. Before connecting to Internet sites, find out how to exit connections.

"Why Isn't This Text Formatted?" Many electronic texts are available on the Internet. When you copy them or receive them from others, the files are usually formatted as "text only." Text-only files do not contain varying fonts, font sizes, and other formatting features. To format these files, you must open them in a word processing program and apply its options (see chapter 5, "Formatting Documents").

16b–4 Helpful hints

As is true of any new technology, the Internet can be frustrating because of the time it takes to learn and use it. Here are some tips for learning to use the Internet efficiently.

Get Help. Do not try to learn the Internet entirely alone. Get help early and whenever you need it. Find a mentor to help you learn and to demonstrate unfamiliar terms and commands. Experienced classmates, co-workers, professors, and friends can be excellent teachers and guides. Technical experts (people who manage the computers you use, for instance) will sometimes make appointments to give you help as you get started. Classes about using the Internet are available at some universities and in other organizations. Manuals, help documents, and other reference materials are also available. FAQ (Frequently Asked Questions) files, online Internet guides, and news groups for new users (see 18c, "News Groups") are all available on the Internet.

Learn in Steps. When you begin, start with one purpose, such as searching for information or using e-mail. Become comfortable with one purpose before trying others. Do not try to learn everything at once. When you begin to understand one key concept, you will more easily learn others.

Find Out the Best Times to Connect. You can spend several minutes each day, equaling hours each month, trying to "connect." If you are dialing in from home, phone lines may be busy. Wait until nonpeak times when fewer people are using your network.

Catalog Useful Internet Sites. When you find useful sites, make a list of their addresses in a separate file. Some Internet applications will "bookmark" Internet addresses permanently so you can return to them easily.

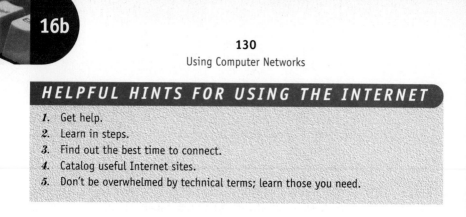

HELPFUL HINTS FOR USING THE INTERNET

1. Get help.
2. Learn in steps.
3. Find out the best time to connect.
4. Catalog useful Internet sites.
5. Don't be overwhelmed by technical terms; learn those you need.

SIMPLIFY TECHNICAL TERMS. Words, phrases, and acronyms that represent technical terms appear in software documentation, reference manuals, on the Internet, and in popular media. Their unfamiliarity may cause you to feel excluded before you even begin using electronic communication, but do not let that stop you. This is not rocket science.

You will learn technical terms you need to know as you explore electronic communication programs and attempt unfamiliar processes. When you hear or read unfamiliar terms, make a note of them to find out what they mean for you, if anything. Ask "What does it do?" and "Do I need to have it do that for me?" These questions help you simplify the range of terms you need to know by connecting them to actions you take.

The Next Time You Write

1. Find out what kinds of computer networks you have access to. What kinds of services and resources do they offer? Do you have Internet access from networks at work or school? Can you access this network from home?

2. Find out how to change your password. If needed, change it to something more secure and more memorable by using combinations of special characters, numbers, and uppercase letters.

3. Locate materials about the Internet at work, school, or a local library, to help you understand the Internet better. Are handouts available? Are classes available?

4. Make a list of questions you have about the Internet. Use them to guide your uses of Internet reference materials.

→ **17** ←

Using the Internet for Research

131

Building on the research strategies in chapter 9, "Research Writing," this chapter describes how you can use various Internet programs to search the world for materials and retrieve them. You will learn about using Telnet to connect to other computers, including libraries from around the world; FTP to copy files from other computers; and Gopher to find directories and files you can use. This chapter also explains how the World Wide Web makes it easier to find and copy information.

17a Connecting to Other Computers

Learning how to use the Internet for detailed research takes time because there are many ways to connect your computer to other computers that provide sources. To gain access to these other computers, you need their addresses, which you can find in various ways. You can make direct connections to the Internet via software like Telnet or you can use the World Wide Web or a commercial Internet access provider to make connections. You can get more information and take classes about these uses of the Internet at a local library, place of employment, or school. You can copy the software you will need to make connections from many Internet sources and purchase it for a nominal fee.

17a–1 Telnet

Telnet programs allow you to connect your computer to other computers by typing in specific computer addresses. These addresses may be in the form of numbers (such as 119.120.32.44) or letters (such as cc.purdue.edu). When you connect to such addresses, you usually will be asked to enter information that identifies you as a registered user of a specific computer system (see 16a–2, "Passwords and security"). When you establish a Telnet connection, a message, a menu, or both will appear. For example, the University of Utah's computer center shows its users the menu in Figure 17.1 when they log in.

17a–2 World Wide Web

Another way to connect to research sources is through the World Wide Web, which allows you to search for the addresses of libraries and to use other connecting programs that find and retrieve sources (see 17b–4, "Combining tasks"). Commercial access providers also support research by providing ways to connect to libraries, file servers, and other research sources.

Figure 17.1 University of Utah's Menu

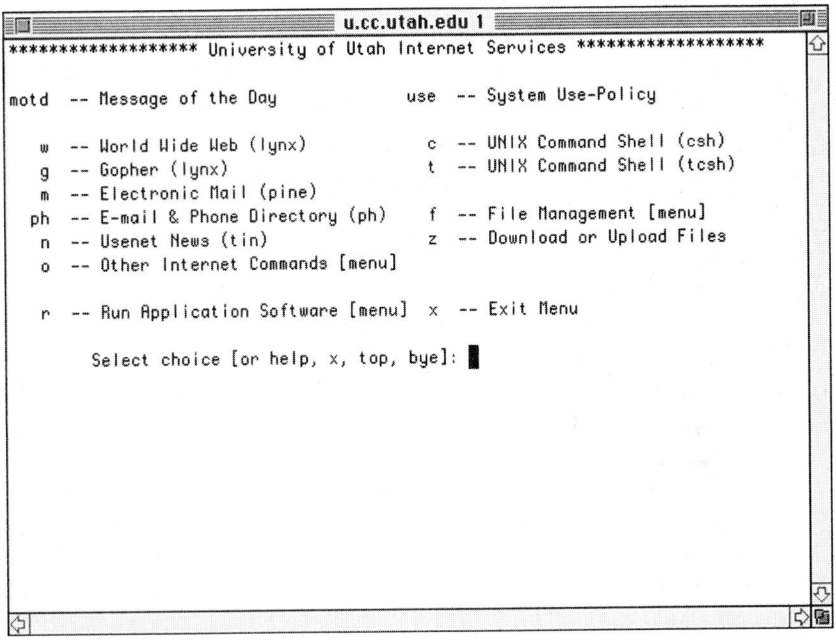

```
┌─────────────────────────────────────────────────────────────────┐
│ ▢▤        u.cc.utah.edu 1                                      ▤ │
│ ******************* University of Utah Internet Services ******************* │
│                                                                   │
│ motd  -- Message of the Day        use  -- System Use-Policy      │
│                                                                   │
│   w  -- World Wide Web (lynx)        c  -- UNIX Command Shell (csh)│
│   g  -- Gopher (lynx)                t  -- UNIX Command Shell (tcsh)│
│   m  -- Electronic Mail (pine)                                    │
│  ph  -- E-mail & Phone Directory (ph)  f  -- File Management [menu]│
│   n  -- Usenet News (tin)            z  -- Download or Upload Files│
│   o  -- Other Internet Commands [menu]                            │
│                                                                   │
│   r  -- Run Application Software [menu]  x  -- Exit Menu           │
│                                                                   │
│      Select choice [or help, x, top, bye]: █                      │
│                                                                   │
│                                                                   │
│                                                                   │
│                                                                   │
└─────────────────────────────────────────────────────────────────┘
```

17b Searching for Information via the Internet

When you want more sources than those you find in a local library's online catalog, database indexes, and electronic texts, you can use the programs described here to connect to other libraries to get files or to request materials through interlibrary loans if you have time when working on a lengthy research project (see 9c, "Obtaining Sources You Need").

17b–1 Kinds of information available

Libraries throughout the world make their online catalogs and other resources available via the Internet. The Internet will give you access to larger libraries that contain vast collections, special holdings of manuscripts, and other archived material. You may find little-known sources by well-known authors; recent, difficult-to-find references; information about regional governments and industries; and other materials that local libraries cannot supply. In addition, you will be able to find pictures, maps, and media sources to transfer to your computer for use in your documents.

17b-2 Finding addresses

The addresses of research sources appear in many places, both on and off the Internet. On the Internet, you will find addresses by using search devices like Yahoo!, AltaVista, and many others that allow you to look for the name of a library (such as "Harvard"), for the name of a source, or for topics to develop. Addresses may also appear in e-mail communications from discussion lists and bulletin boards. When you read journals and magazines, you may also see addresses of useful electronic sources.

17b-3 Gopher

Gopher programs greatly simplify the process of finding information on the Internet because they index topics in relation to specific computer addresses. Gopher programs are commonly available on the menus of many computer systems, where they show indexes of specific types of information. You can browse through a list of topics like "arts," "reference," "weather," and many others. Gopher programs connect to Gopher servers, computers that contain indexes of information and links to still other servers. When you learn of an available file or directory listing you need on a Gopher server, find out the following:

● What is the server's address?

● What is the name of the directory where the file is located?

● What is the file name?

After you enter a Gopher address and connect, you may see a welcome message. Press Enter, and the next screen will list directories. These directories take you to subdirectories or files and are sometimes linked to other servers. Gopher programs also allow you to search Gopher servers around the world by entering key words.

If you are using a Gopher program that displays text only, use arrow keys or numbers to highlight a directory, then press Enter to select it. If you are using a Gopher program that displays icons for directories, simply double-click on an icon to access further directories or files.

17b-4 Combining tasks (World Wide Web)

The World Wide Web (also called WWW, W3, or Web) combines the functions of connecting to other computers, copying files, and searching the Internet for information. With software that "browses the Web" (such as Netscape), you can access not only electronic documents that are on the Web, but FTP and Gopher servers and their documents as well. Most Web browsers will also open Telnet connections, send e-mail, and access news groups. Therefore, you can use a Web browser as your interface with the Internet—using it to access various types of sites all over the world.

Figure 17.2 Gopher Program for Windows

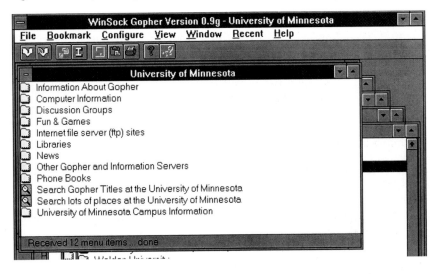

To access Internet sites with the Web, you must use the appropriate address. Combining additional prefixes to Internet addresses makes up what is called a URL. Table 17.1 lists some examples of URLs.

The initials http stand for "hypertext transfer protocol"—the language that Web browsers interpret to display text, pictures, and "hypertext" links. By selecting or clicking on highlighted text or graphics on a Web screen, you can activate a hypertext link, which connects you to another Web page or Internet site or allows you to send e-mail, download sound or video clips, or launch other Internet programs.

TABLE 17.1 SAMPLE UNIFORM RESOURCE LOCATORS (URLS)		
What do you want to do?	**Use this Prefix**	**Type the Prefix and the Internet Address (the URL)** **For example**
Connect to an FTP Server	ftp://	ftp://ftp.dartmouth.edu
Connect to a Gopher Server	gopher://	gopher://gopher.tc.umn.edu
Connect to a WWW server	http://	http://www.yahoo.com
Open a Telnet connection	telnet://	telnet://infogate.lib.utah.edu
Send e-mail	mailto:	mailto:greg.willard@davis.edu
Access a News Group	news:	news:misc.writing.screenplays

When you access a Web site (by typing a URL), the first screen you see is called a "home page" (sometimes called a "welcome page"). The home page is the first of possibly several related Web pages at a particular Web site.

Most Web browsers allow you to see pictures as well as text, play sounds, and view video clips. Links are usually highlighted in a different color and underlined. A small number of browsers (such as Lynx for Unix users) do not display pictures, play sounds, or allow you to view video clips, but simply display text and highlight hypertext links.

17b–5 Hytelnet

Hytelnet is a program that allows you to find a particular library's Internet address. When you search with a Gopher program or the World Wide Web (see 17b, "Searching for Information," and 17b–4, "Combining tasks"), you can link directly to libraries or you can note the Internet addresses of libraries for later use.

The easiest way to find library Internet addresses is by connecting to the Hytelnet Web page. Hytelnet is a catalog of library and other Internet addresses from around the world. Hytelnet not only displays the addresses, but will open a Telnet connection for you. You can use a Web browser (see 17b–4, "Combining tasks") either to copy the Hytelnet program from http://www.lights.com/hytelnet/ or connect to the Hytelnet Web page at http://moondog.usask.ca/hytelnet/.

If you wanted to look for sources at the Harvard University library, for example, you would follow these steps:

1. Use a Web browser to connect to http://moondog.usask.ca/hytelnet/.

2. Click (or, if using a text-based browser, use arrow keys) to select "Library catalogs, arranged geographically."

3. Click on "The Americas."

4. Click on "United States /By State."

5. Click on "Massachusetts."

6. Click on "Harvard University."

7. The screen in Figure 17.3 appears.

8. If your system opens multiple applications simultaneously, you can click on the Telnet address (hollis.harvard.edu) to open a Telnet connection to the library while your Web connection remains active. Otherwise, make a note of the Telnet address, quit your Web browser, and open a Telnet connection to hollis.harvard.edu. Once connected, type "hollis."

9. The screen in Figure 17.4 appears. You are connected to Harvard's online library system.

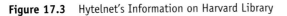

Figure 17.3 Hytelnet's Information on Harvard Library

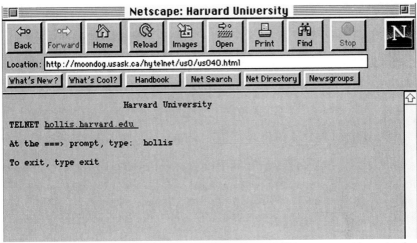

17c Retrieving Information from the Internet

As you conduct research on the Internet, you will find the names and locations of documents you want to quote or refer to extensively. You may want the electronic text of a literary work, an important article, or a visual source to illustrate your points. You can transfer these files to your computer and send files to other computers from yours.

Figure 17.4 Telnet Connection to Harvard's Online Library

```
** HOLLIS **

                          WELCOME TO HOLLIS
                 Harvard OnLine Library Information System


HU   Union Catalog of the Harvard     AI   Expanded Academic Index, 1987-
     libraries                        AL   Anthropological Literature, 1983-
OW   Catalog of Older Widener         ER   ERIC, 1989-
     materials                        LR   Legal Resource Index, 1980-
RV   Course Reserves Database         PA   PAIS International, 1985-
LG   Guide to Harvard Libraries       PP   Physics Pre-prints, 1991-
                                      PS   PsycINFO, 1984-
                                      RI   ATLA Religion Index, 1949-
                                      RS   RISM, Music Manuscripts 1580-1825


To select a database from any place in HOLLIS, type CHOOSE followed by a
2-character database code, as in:   CHOOSE HU   and press ENTER or RETURN.

For general help in using HOLLIS, type HELP now. Type EXIT to disconnect.
For HOLLIS news, type HELP NEWS.

COMMAND? ▊
```

17c-1 Copying files (FTP)

Using specialized FTP ("file transfer protocol") programs, you can connect to file servers to copy files to and from your computer. Files contained on FTP servers may be text, pictures, or software. When a Gopher search or another source identifies material you want from an FTP server, find out the following:

● What is the address?

● What is the name of the directory where the file is located?

● What is the file name?

FTP programs (such as Fetch or Windows FTP) make it easy to copy files from one computer to another. These programs allow you to connect and reconnect to frequently visited FTP sites by putting their addresses in lists called "bookmarks" or "shortcuts." Clicking on a bookmark or short-cut automatically displays a site's list of files and directories through which

Figure 17.5   Fetch: FTP Program for Macintosh

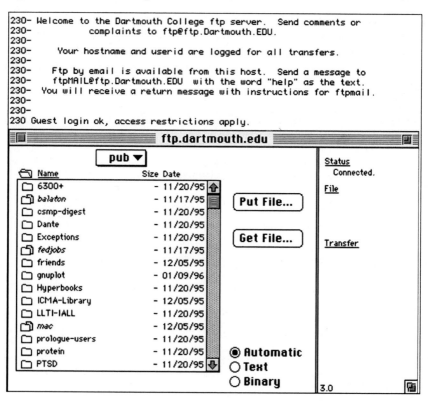

you can search with a mouse. When you find a file you want to copy, you simply double-click on its name.

To connect to an FTP site without using an FTP program's bookmark or shortcut, you can use Telnet or another connecting program. After you type in a specific FTP server's address, you usually will be asked to enter an account name and password. If a publicly accessible site requires login information, try entering "anonymous" or "guest" as the account name. Many libraries and other information sites have publicly accessible computers that do not require individual logins or passwords. When prompted for a password, press Enter. Sometimes a site will accept your e-mail address as the password.

One publicly accessible FTP site (or "anonymous FTP server") is Dartmouth College's FTP server. You can copy software and electronic texts from a Dartmouth archive named Dante. To do so, first open an FTP connection with Telnet, to ftp.dartmouth.edu. Enter "anonymous" as the login name. After you enter your e-mail address as the password, you will see a welcome message and an FTP prompt (ftp>). At the prompt, you will need to enter commands that allow you to view available files and retrieve them.

17c–2 Common FTP commands

You must type commands to find and copy files when you use Telnet or other text-based FTP programs to connect to an FTP server. For instance, "dir" is a command related to "directory," a list of names of files. (At Dartmouth, Dante is a directory name.) When you identify the name of a file you want to copy, you will most commonly use the command "get" plus the file name to retrieve it. Here is a list of useful commands.

ascii: sets ftp to a "text" (text only) transfer mode, the most common way to transfer files

binary: sets ftp to "binary" mode, which is necessary for copying pictures, software programs, and other files that are not text only

bye: ends your ftp connection (sometimes exit or quit)

cd [directory.name]: change directory (for example, "cd pub.mac" means "change directory to 'public access for Macintosh'")

cd ..: shifts the file names you see down one directory level

dir: shows what is in the current folder or directory (also "ls")

get [file.name]: copies a file from the server to your computer

put [file.name]: copies a file from your computer to the server

user: FTP servers do not always request account information when you connect, but entering "user" will bring up a request for your account name and password.

17d Electronic Books

Telnet, Gopher, FTP, and Web browsers connect you not only to indexed lists of electronic texts but to the texts themselves. Many books and articles are available in electronic files. For example, the complete works of Shakespeare with hypertext links and search capabilities are located at MIT's Shakespeare Web page (http://the-tech.mit.edu/Shakespeare/works.html).

Other projects that make electronic texts available on the Internet include Project Gutenberg and Project Bartleby.

Figure 17.6 Shakespeare's Works on the Web

Project Gutenberg's goal is to provide electronic versions of ten thousand of the most used books by the year 2001. You can read the group's newuser.gut file and download electronic texts by making an FTP connection to ftp://uiarchive.cso.uiuc.edu/pub/etext/gutenberg.

Project Bartleby, from the Bartleby Library at Columbia University, has the goal of providing accurate editions, free public access, careful selections, and state-of-the-art presentation. Texts already on the Internet include *The Elements of Style* and poems by Emily Dickinson and Robert Frost. You can access Project Bartleby on the Web at http://www.columbia.edu/acis/bartleby/index.html.

When you find electronic texts and copy them to your computer, you can open them in your word processing program, select passages you want to quote in your writing, and search for specific words and phrases.

Books on the Internet are often out of copyright, but you must still cite them in your own work the way you would cite any source material. Individual documents published only electronically should never be used without citation (see 7d, "Notes from Sources").

The Next Time You Write

1. Connect to some Internet sites used as examples in this chapter. For example, try using an FTP program to connect to Project Gutenberg (ftp://uiarchive.cso.uiuc.edu/pub/etext/gutenberg). Find a text to copy and copy it to your computer. Open it in your word processing program.

2. Use your World Wide Web browser to access an FTP site and a Gopher site. For example, in the "Open Connection" or Internet address field, type: ftp://uiarchive.cso.uiuc.edu/pub/etext/gutenberg. When you are connected, click or select links that take you to directories or files. See if your Web browser can send e-mail and access news groups.

3. Find an Internet address for a library in another state. Try connecting to it using a Telnet program and practice searching through its online catalog.

4. Retrieve an electronic text (a chapter or portion) from Project Gutenberg or Project Bartleby (see 17d, "Electronic Books"). Copy it into your word processor. Review conventions for citing electronic sources (see 9c-3, "Checking and citing electronic sources").

PART FOUR

Many Writers, Many Computers

18

Connecting with Other Writers

18a

This chapter describes how to converse with other writers using electronic connections. It discusses using electronic mail (e-mail), participating in e-mail discussion groups (mailing lists), participating in news groups, and participating in real-time conversations over the Internet.

18a Electronic Mail (e-mail)

E-mail is an easy way to send messages to friends, to contact organizations, to write letters to the editor, and to get comments on your documents from readers. E-mail correspondents can get messages and reply almost instantaneously, so you can also use e-mail to schedule meetings and arrange telephone conversations without time-consuming phone tag.

18a-1 Your address

When you obtain an account on a network with access to the Internet, you will also receive an e-mail address. E-mail addresses have three or more parts, separated by @ and by periods: your e-mail name, the name of the computer that "serves" your e-mail, and the type of organization of that server. For example, lcrosby@ohio.edu is an address for someone named Linda Crosby. Everything after the @ symbol is called the "domain name"; "ohio.edu" is Ohio University's domain name ("edu" is used for an educational organization). The following are typical organizational domain abbreviations:

edu (educational)

com (commercial)

gov (government)

mil (military)

org (nonprofit organization)

net (network service)

There are many geographical domains, such as "uk" for England, "de" for Germany (Deutscheland), "ie" for Ireland, and "au" for Australia.

E-mail addresses must be typed precisely, or your messages will be returned with an "unknown user" error message.

Many organizations have online phone directories located on their Gopher server or Web server (see chapter 17, "Using the Internet for Research"). These often include e-mail addresses. You can add your own address to Web sites that have large e-mail directories. Two sites are the Internet Address Finder at http://www.iaf.net and the Four11 White Page Directory at http://www.four11.com.

18a–2 E-mail header information

E-mail message screens have spaces ("fields") where you identify the address of the person you are writing to and indicate whether you are attaching files to your message.

TO.   On this line, type the e-mail address of the primary person or persons to whom you are writing. For example, if you were writing to the President of the United States, you would type president@whitehouse.gov. If you are writing to more than one person or list, separate the e-mail addresses with a comma and a space. (See 18a–3, "Helpful hints.")

CC: AND BCC:.   Carbon copy (Cc:) and blind carbon copy (Bcc:) are used to send copies of e-mail to another person or persons. For example, if you wanted to thank a co-worker for a job well done, you could type your supervisor's e-mail address in the Cc: field. Your appreciation would then also go to your supervisor. Use Bcc: on the rare occasions when you send copies of messages to people without the primary correspondent's knowledge.

ATTACHMENTS.   Most e-mail programs allow you to send entire computer files with e-mail messages, either by attaching the files or by copying and pasting the text, without formatting, into the message.

To send formatted word processing files, you need to know if your e-mail program will automatically compress and code files so they can be sent over the Internet. If your e-mail software does not do this automatically, you can use programs like UUEncode or PKZip on the PC and StuffIt Deluxe or CompactPro on the Mac. You can get such programs from the Web at http://www.shareware.com.

Figure 18.1   E-mail Header Information

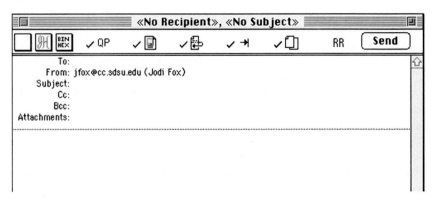

Always include a brief message with attached files, specifying the original file format (such as WordPerfect 5.1 for DOS, MS Word 6.0 for Macintosh) and saying how the file is compressed (for example, UUEncoded). Some compression programs allow you to save the file as a "self-extracting" (.sea) file, so the person receiving it simply has to open it to decode and decompress it. Others require that the person receiving it have a program to decode and uncompress it.

If you and your recipient do not need to keep the original formatting of a document, you can save it as "text only," a format that can be opened by any e-mail or word processing program.

SUBJECT. In this space, type a short description of your message. This description should define the purpose of your message, much like a title of a paper or report. A person receiving e-mail usually sees only the subject line and the name of the sender in a list of incoming messages, so your subject should specifically say what your message is about. "Please Renew," for instance, is more specific than "Library Books, " and "Removing Cat Hair" is more informative than "Filthy Felines!" Specific, informative subjects make it easier to locate messages.

18a–3 Helpful hints

Opinions vary about how to write e-mail messages. Some readers are unforgiving about spelling and grammatical errors, while others accept e-mail as an informal way of communicating and do not worry about spelling and grammar. But here are some general e-mail guidelines you should always follow.

Be a responsible e-mail user. Follow the e-mail policies and procedures distributed by your system administrator. Remember that e-mail may be monitored. *Never* leave your computer before logging off (quitting) your network account. Make backup copies of e-mail messages you wish to save.

Write formal messages in a word processing program first. If you write to a friend, formality probably is not important. But if you write to a business associate or to request information from a professional source, for instance, keep in mind the impression your writing will make.

In these and other formal situations, use a word processing program to produce a polished text. You can then copy and paste the text from your word processing file into your e-mail message, or you can attach the file to the message (see 18a–2, "E-mail header information").

Write pointed, brief messages. Focus on the purpose that you identify on the subject line. If you want to take up multiple subjects, consider writing separate messages about each one. Break up the text of a long message, separating brief paragraphs with double spacing to help readers scan your message quickly.

Use only a few abbreviations. Many common e-mail abbreviations may be unfamiliar to your readers, such as "btw" (by the way) and "imo" (in my opinion). In regular correspondence with one person, you can develop mutual ways to abbreviate. But avoid unfamiliar terms unless you know your reader appreciates their brevity.

Include a signature and contact information. Some e-mail programs allow you to create and save a signature file containing your "signature" and contact information. This file is automatically inserted into your messages every time you write. If your e-mail program does not have this feature, create your own signature file to open and copy into messages. But limit your signature to three or four lines.

When writing to strangers, it is important to include a signature at the end of messages. Include phone and fax numbers with your address.

Reply to e-mail quickly. If an e-mail message requires a response, reply as soon as possible. In your reply, include the requested information and answer questions. Many e-mail programs have a "reply" feature that automatically starts a new message addressed to the original sender. If you tell it to do so, this feature will copy the original message into your new message with ">" or ":" at the beginning of each line of the original message. Use the original message to outline a response, but quote from it only where it makes your reply clearer.

Use address books. Most e-mail programs allow you to create address books that list addresses, sometimes called "nicknames." Instead of typing a friend's address every time you send a message, you can call up his or her address book entry. You might enter the nickname "james," for instance, to represent james.ellis@cc.msu.edu. Nicknames can represent one e-mail address or multiple e-mail addresses (sometimes called distribution lists).

Do not rely on e-mail. Networks can go down and e-mail may be delayed or lost for technical reasons. If your message is important, send e-mail and call the person, fax, or send a printed copy of the message.

Figure 18.2   E-mail Signature

```
Thank you for your interest in applying to Florida State University.

The application materials you requested are going out in today's mail.

Good Luck!

Kari Wright

----------------------------------------------------------------------------
Kari Wright, Admissions Clerk
Florida State University - PO Box 2175 - Tallahassee, FL 32316 - (904) 487-6318
----------------------------------------------------------------------------
```

18b Mailing Lists

Mailing lists (sometimes called discussion lists or LISTSERVs) are e-mail groups set up for discussions of specific topics. Messages sent to one e-mail address are distributed to everyone who "subscribes" to the list. Some lists have moderators who read messages before they are distributed to check that they fit the mailing list's objectives.

Mailing lists have two e-mail addresses:

1. A LISTSERV address where you subscribe to and unsubscribe from the mailing list (for example, listserv@mitvma.mit.edu). The LISTSERV address usually begins with "listserv" but sometimes begins with "majordomo," "listproc," or other names. LISTSERV is one of the programs used to create and manage mailing lists.

2. An address of a mailing list where you send messages to be distributed to the list's subscribers (for example, writers@mitvma.mit.edu). Table 18.1 contains examples of LISTSERV and mailing list addresses of interest to writers.

You can also use e-mail to subscribe to electronic publication mailing lists. These lists are distributed daily, weekly, or monthly by various organizations. For example, "Edupage," a summary of news items on information technology, is sent three times a week to the e-mail addresses of several thousand subscribers.

For more addresses, check http://www.neosoft.com/internet/paml/ for publicly accessible mailing lists, or http://www.earn.net/lug/notice.html for a LISTSERV user's guide.

To subscribe to a mailing list, first find its LISTSERV address. Send an e-mail message to the LISTSERV address, typing in the body of the message only "sub [listname] [your name]." Type nothing in the subject line. For example, if Michelle Rodriguez wanted to subscribe to the Rhetoric, Language, and Professional Writing list, she would address a message to listserv@vm.cc.purdue.edu. Then she would type "sub purtopoi Michelle Rodriguez" in the body of the message.

You will receive an e-mail message from the mailing list when your subscription is processed. This message usually contains instructions on how to unsubscribe from the list and gives guidelines for writing messages to the group. Save this message for future reference.

Warning: Daily messages from mailing lists can overload your e-mail account and waste your time. Subscribe only to one or two lists at a time; decide whether a mailing list is useful and if you have time to keep up with its messages. Remember to unsubscribe from mailing lists when you will be away from e-mail for an extended period.

TABLE 18.1 MAILING LISTS FOR WRITERS

Name	LISTSERV Address	Mailing List Address
Composition Digest	listserv@ulkyvx.louisville.edu	compos01@ulkyvx.louisville.edu
Creative Writing Pedagogy for Teachers and Students	listserv@umcvmb.missouri.edu	crewrt-l@umcvmb.missouri.edu
History of Rhetoric	listserv@ uicvm.uic.edu	h-rhetor@ uicvm.uic.edu
Online Journalism Seminar	listserv@cmuvm.csv.cmich.edu	jrntut-a@cmuvm.csv.cmich.edu
Workshop for Poetry	listserv@gsuvm1.bitnet	poet-l@gsuvm1.binet
Rhetoric, Language, and Professional Writing	listserv@vm.cc.purdue.edu	purtopoi@vm.cc.purdue.edu
Cyberjournal for Rhetoric and Writing	listserv@mizzou1.missouri.edu	rhetnt-1@mizzou1.missouri.edu
Screenwriting Discussion List	listserv@tamvm1.bitnet	scrnwrit@tamvm1.bitnet
Technical Communication Issues	listserv@vm1.ucc.okstate.edu	techwr-l@vm1.ucc.okstate.edu
Fiction Writers Workshop	listserv@psuvm.psu.edu	fiction@psuvm.psu.edu

18c News Groups

News groups are Internet places for exchanging messages about specific topics. Unlike mailing lists, which send messages to an individual's e-mail address, messages written for news groups are "posted" to the news group

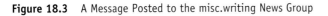

Figure 18.3   A Message Posted to the misc.writing News Group

```
╔═══════════════════ All Newsgroups ═══════════════════╗
 Unread  All  Newsgroup
              misc.transport.rail.misc
              misc.transport.road
              misc.transport.trucking                        ▶
              misc.transport.urban-transit
              misc.wanted
 ● 1053 1054  misc.writing
              misc.writing.screenplays
              news.admin.censorship
              news.admin.hierarchies
              news.admin.misc
              news.admin.net-abuse.announce
              news.admin.net-abuse.misc
 Unread  All  Topics in: misc.writing
 ●    2     2  Re: Save the Rats!!! Was
 ●    1     1  FAQ -- your questions about writing answered
 ●    1     1  FAQ -- posting guidelines for misc.writing
 ●   12    12  Re: What happened to Mingo?
 ●    1     1  Need Advice on Book Proposal
 ●    3     3  Re: Multiple Timelines
 ●    1     1  Any expert writers?
 ●    1     1  Re: A Writer's Lament
 ●    1     1  Re: "interviewing" agents
 ●    1     1  Re: need a bit of help (with chocolate)
 ●    1     1  editor needed
 ●    1     1  Environmental fiction
 ●    1     1  Skylite Magazine WRITERS WANTED
 ●    1     1  SKYLITE MAGAZINE ADDRESS
 ●    3     3  Re: Naming the ****ing characters!
 ● 53922  editor needed                           Liza Pagano
 Online fashion magazine seeks editor

 Fashion Internet is looking for a features editor, to start late June.

 Duties include:

 * Work with fashion editor and art director to conceptualize and
 produce 10-20 pieces a month.

 * Seek out and commission freelance writers, editors, animators,
 photographers, and videofolk.

 * Act as developmental/line editor on all features and other
 assorted articles.

 * Copyedit all text on site.
```

address. Using newsreader software (such as tin, InterNews, NewsWatcher, or Web browsers), you can read and write messages for news groups.

Newsreader software programs connect you to a news server where all of the news groups and messages are stored. Depending on how your news server is administered, you may be able to access all or only some of the more than ten thousand news groups available.

News group addresses are named with prefixes that identify general subjects. These prefixes are followed by more specific information about the group. Table 18.2 lists some popular news group prefixes along with examples of news group addresses.

There are many other news group prefixes. Organizations often set up their own news groups with their own prefixes. Often these news groups can be accessed only by members of the organization.

Here are some news groups that discuss writing: alt.usage.english, comp.edu.composition, misc.writing, misc.writing.screenplays, rec.music.makers.songwriting.

You can find out more about newsgroups at http://www.cen.uiuc.edu/cgi-bin/find-news or http://sunsite.unc.edu/usenet-i/.

TABLE 18.2 COMMON NEWS GROUP PREFIXES

Prefix	Subjects	Example
alt	alternative	alt.adoption
biz	business	biz.jobs.offered
clari	ClariNet	clari.apbl.tv
comp	computers	comp.publish.cdrom.multimedia
misc	miscellaneous	misc.writing.screenplays
news	newsgroups	news.answers
rec	recreation	rec.arts.startrek.fandom
sci	science	sci.archaeology
soc	society	soc.retirement

18d Hints for Using Mailing Lists and News Groups

● Read the mailing list's or new group's FAQ (Frequently Asked Questions) file before sending or posting messages.

● Use the LISTSERV address (not the mailing list address) to subscribe to and unsubscribe from mailing lists.

● Use descriptive subject titles for your messages.

● Keep messages short and related to your subject title.

● Limit your signature to three or four lines.

● Send replies to individual e-mail addresses when appropriate instead of to the mailing list or news group.

18e Real-time Conversation on the Internet

The Internet makes it possible to simulate telephone and conference conversations where people talk face to face. The programs discussed in this section allow you to carry on real-time conversations with other Internet users.

18e–1 Talk and Chat

Talk is a program that allows you to communicate directly with another person on the Internet by typing alternately at the same time. Once connected, you will see a split screen. One portion displays your writing and the other displays the writing of the other person.

Figure 18.4   Example of a Real-time Talk Session

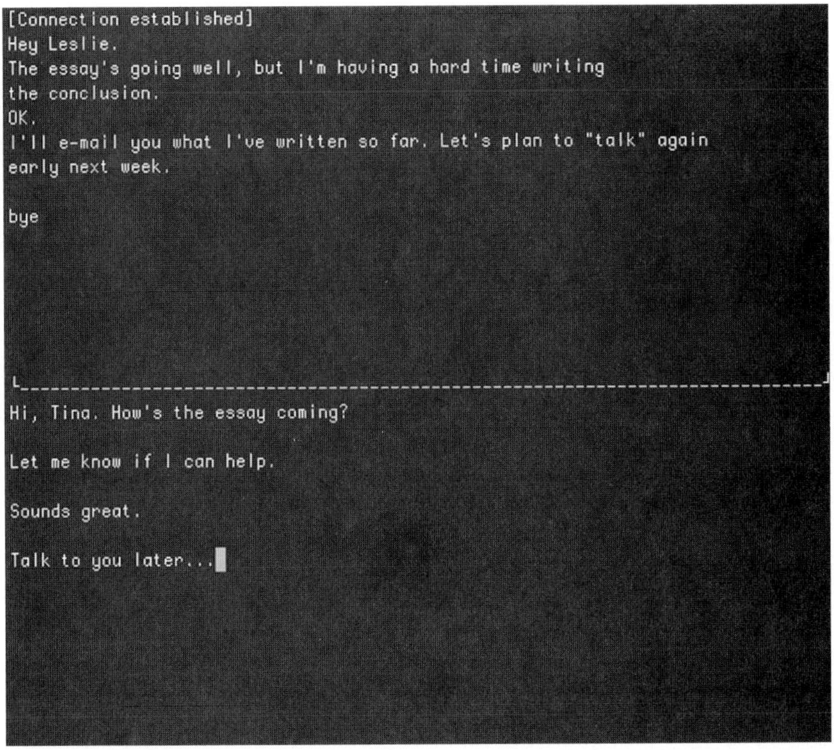

```
[Connection established]
Hey Leslie.
The essay's going well, but I'm having a hard time writing
the conclusion.
OK.
I'll e-mail you what I've written so far. Let's plan to "talk" again
early next week.

bye



L_____

Hi, Tina. How's the essay coming?

Let me know if I can help.

Sounds great.

Talk to you later...█
```

Some networks allow you to initiate a talk session by typing "talk [e-mail address]" after a command prompt (such as csh> or n:>). For example, if your friend's e-mail address is kathy@asu.edu, you would type "talk kathy@asu.edu" at the command prompt. If Kathy is logged in to her account at the time, she will receive a "request for talk" message and possibly instructions on how to establish the connection. Remember: System administrators may or may not allow talk to work on their network, or they may limit the hours for talk sessions. Check with them for further instructions.

To hold a discussion with more than one person, you can use a similar program called chat. Chat programs allow users to connect to organized electronic conversations about various subjects. For example, if your system administrator created a forum to discuss the Super Bowl, you could connect to it by typing "chat superbowl" at the command prompt. Once connected, you type messages to other users that they see after you press the Enter key. Check with system administrators for the availability of chat discussions.

18e-2 Internet Relay Chat (IRC)

Internet Relay Chat (IRC) is a program that allows many people on the Internet to meet to discuss various subjects. Using Telnet or specialized IRC programs (such as Homer), you can connect to IRC servers (such as irc2.texas.net). IRC servers manage IRC channels. Channel names always begin with # (#soccer, #u2, #writing).

After you connect to an IRC server, type "/list" to see available channels. It may take a long time to display the entire list of channels, so be patient. If you find a channel you would like to join, use the "/join [#channel]" command. Each time users type text and press the Enter key, their messages are displayed to others connected to the channel.

IRC COMMANDS.   Here is a short list of useful IRC commands:

/**help**: to see commands you can learn to use

/**join [#channel]**: to join a channel

/**list**: to list available channels

/**nick**: to change your nickname

/**quit**: to quit irc

/**topic [topic]**: to change the topic of a channel

/**who [#channel]**: to see who is on a channel

/**whois ***: to show more information about everyone on a channel

/**whois [name]**: to show more information about a particular user

Figure 18.5   An Internet Relay Chat (IRC) Session

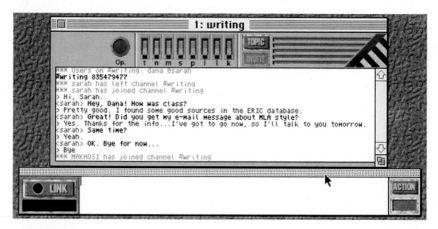

Many IRC servers include a "#writing" channel or other writing-related channels. When connected to an IRC server, you can type "/join #writing" to create a new discussion of writing or any other topic.

For more information about IRCs, see http://www.uai.cl/~burton/servers/, http://www.botree.co.uk/library/irc.htm, or the IRC news group at alt.irc.

18e-3 Multiple User Domains (MUDs)

Multiple user domains (MUDs) combine the features of talk, chat, and IRC. But MUDs add an additional dimension to Internet conversations. MUDs are virtual textual worlds. Not only can you talk with others, but you can move around rooms, view descriptions of objects, and perform actions. Most MUDs are role-playing fantasy or science fiction games, but educational and professional MUDs are also available. These are also known as MOOs.

Using Telnet or specialized MUD programs, you can connect to a MUD server. Once you connect, you see a welcome screen with information about the MUD; it may describe the imagined physical space you are entering.

Once connected, you assume an identity, called a "character." You can specify a new name, a gender, and a brief textual description of your character by using the @describe me command. Sometimes the MUD allows you to join as a guest character; other times you must register your character via e-mail before entering the MUD.

Figure 18.6a Login Screen for a MUD Session

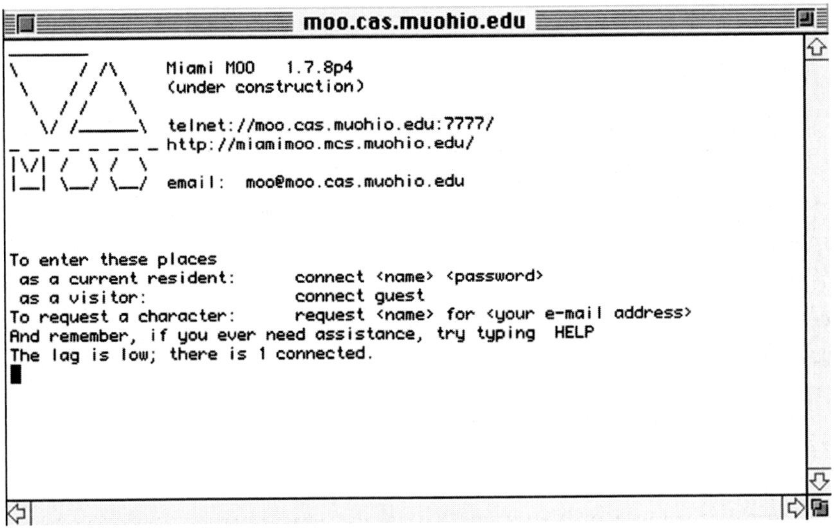

Figure 18.6b   Description Screen for a MUD Session

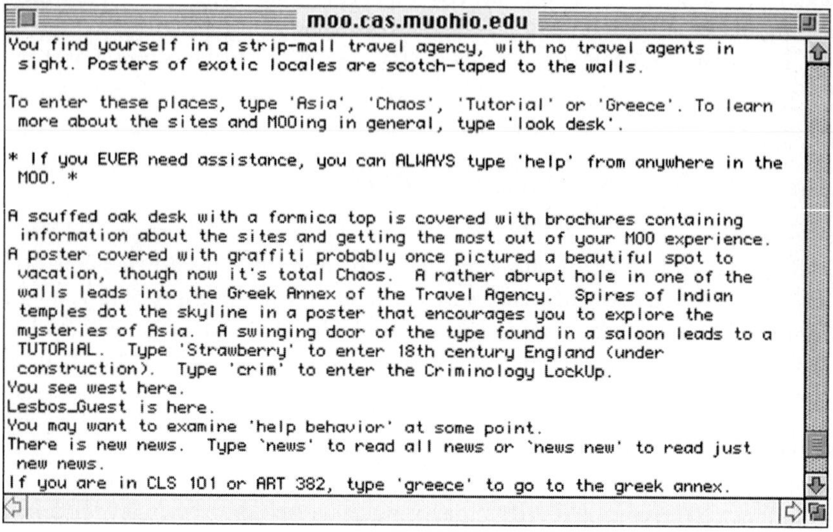

```
moo.cas.muohio.edu

You find yourself in a strip-mall travel agency, with no travel agents in
sight. Posters of exotic locales are scotch-taped to the walls.

To enter these places, type 'Asia', 'Chaos', 'Tutorial' or 'Greece'. To learn
more about the sites and MOOing in general, type 'look desk'.

* If you EVER need assistance, you can ALWAYS type 'help' from anywhere in the
  MOO. *

A scuffed oak desk with a formica top is covered with brochures containing
 information about the sites and getting the most out of your MOO experience.
A poster covered with graffiti probably once pictured a beautiful spot to
 vacation, though now it's total Chaos. A rather abrupt hole in one of the
 walls leads into the Greek Annex of the Travel Agency.  Spires of Indian
 temples dot the skyline in a poster that encourages you to explore the
 mysteries of Asia. A swinging door of the type found in a saloon leads to a
 TUTORIAL.  Type 'Strawberry' to enter 18th century England (under
 construction). Type 'crim' to enter the Criminology LockUp.
You see west here.
Lesbos_Guest is here.
You may want to examine 'help behavior' at some point.
There is new news. Type `news' to read all news or `news new' to read just
 new news.
If you are in CLS 101 or ART 382, type 'greece' to go to the greek annex.
```

Figure 18.6c   Movement in a MUD Session

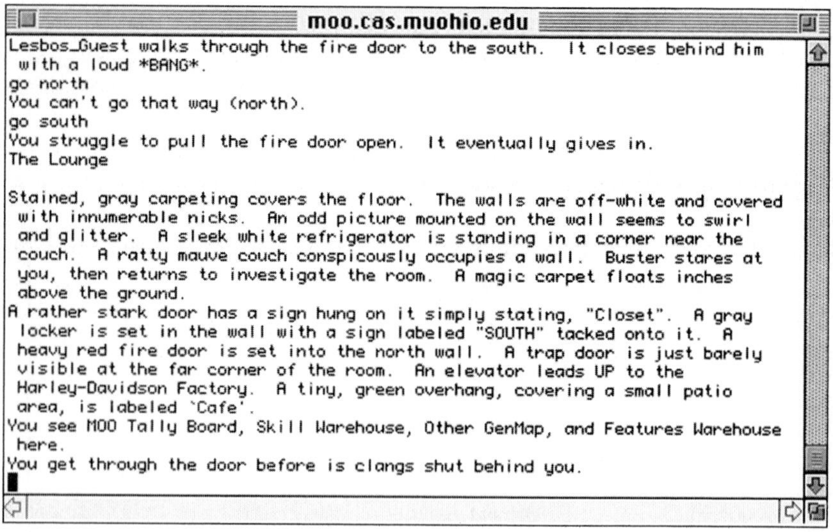

```
moo.cas.muohio.edu

Lesbos_Guest walks through the fire door to the south.  It closes behind him
 with a loud *BANG*.
go north
You can't go that way (north).
go south
You struggle to pull the fire door open. It eventually gives in.
The Lounge

Stained, gray carpeting covers the floor.  The walls are off-white and covered
 with innumerable nicks.  An odd picture mounted on the wall seems to swirl
 and glitter.  A sleek white refrigerator is standing in a corner near the
 couch.  A ratty mauve couch conspicously occupies a wall.  Buster stares at
 you, then returns to investigate the room.  A magic carpet floats inches
 above the ground.
A rather stark door has a sign hung on it simply stating, "Closet".  A gray
 locker is set in the wall with a sign labeled "SOUTH" tacked onto it.  A
 heavy red fire door is set into the north wall.  A trap door is just barely
 visible at the far corner of the room.  An elevator leads UP to the
 Harley-Davidson Factory.  A tiny, green overhang, covering a small patio
 area, is labeled `Cafe'.
You see MOO Tally Board, Skill Warehouse, Other GenMap, and Features Warehouse
 here.
You get through the door before is clangs shut behind you.
```

MUD COMMANDS.   Here is a short list of useful MUD commands.

@describe me: to change your character description

act [action]: to express an action

help: to display the help screen

look [object]: to get a textual description of an object

look: to get the textual description of a room

news: to display information or announcements

quit: to end your MUD session

say [text]: to display your comments

who: to list other players

WRITING MUDS. A few MUDs are devoted to exploring and discussing writing. For instance, universities may have online writing labs (OWLs) where students and guests can discuss their writing with writing instructors and other writers. Search Gopher and Web servers for addresses to local online writing labs.

You can find out more about MUDs at http://www.cis.upenn.edu/~lwl/mudinfo.html or at the MUD news group alt.mud.

The Next Time You Write

1. Subscribe to a mailing list that looks interesting. Then unsubscribe and resubscribe to practice sending messages.

2. Search through news groups to find one you would like to join. Practice posting news group messages to alt.test or misc.test before posting to other news groups.

3. Ask your system administrators about available talk and chat technologies. Send e-mail to others who will help you test those that your system supports.

4. Use the addresses in this chapter to search the Internet for more information on talk, IRCs, and MUDs. What features of these communication programs appeal to you? How could you use them to improve your writing?

→ **19** ←
Using E-mail to Improve Your Writing

This chapter describes how e-mail can be used in various ways to improve your writing. You will learn about using e-mail to write messages to yourself, to ask questions about your writing-in-progress, and to give yourself and others feedback on writing. It emphasizes controlling the tone and style of your e-mail.

19a Messages to Yourself

E-mail can help you practice and control your writing process. Its usual brevity makes it a convenient way to practice simultaneous thinking and writing with a computer. In addition, dated e-mail messages may be saved as records of the progress of a particular project.

E-mail can transfer writing-in-progress for relatively quick, helpful responses and direct comments on a text. You can begin writing in e-mail to imagine your reader more vividly and later move your drafting to a word processing file. E-mail makes it convenient to read unfinished texts, so it encourages you to identify problems and possibilities for improvement.

19b Asking Questions

E-mail makes it easy to try out ideas for writing and to share your drafts with readers, to get help before you write, and to ask quick questions about your ideas or engage in longer exchanges in which you develop your thinking. Using e-mail to ask for help allows you to view your writing from a distance. By pausing to write questions, you become aware of choices you can control about what to say and how to say it. You can pause while you are focusing on a topic to consider readers' knowledge and prior opinions and when you have questions about what to say, how to edit, and how to format a document.

19b–1 Places to ask questions

SOURCES FOR FACTS.   You might write a quick note to a discussion list or news group to get specific facts or information about a project: "I'm writing about baseball—does anyone know M. Mantle's lifetime batting average?" "Where can I find a text of Martin Luther King's 'I Have a Dream' speech on the Internet?" "What is the population of Paris?"

SOURCES FOR THINKING ABOUT TOPICS.   E-mail is a way to develop ideas by corresponding with people thinking along similar lines. If you have an e-mail address for a writer interested in your topic, which you may be able

GUIDELINES FOR ASKING QUESTIONS VIA E-MAIL

1. Place specific questions at the beginning of the message.
2. Ask specific questions that clarify how you want your correspondent to help you.
3. Use disagreements as guides to issues you need to raise and points you need to make in your writing.
4. Put brackets or space around the specific passages about which you have questions or doubts.
5. Save your questions and the answers to them.
6. Be sure your correspondent has time and access to answer e-mail.
7. Attach a file or copy it into your message, depending on your correspondent's system.
8. Make appointments to talk to your readers online.

to find in phone books for educational organizations and in popular publications, you can ask questions and float your ideas for comment. Questions about ideas help you check sources and evidence while they make your interest known among people knowledgeable about your topic.

PEOPLE WITH SIMILAR GOALS. If you're involved in a group writing assignment, use e-mail to exchange ideas about it. You can discuss your topic cooperatively from different perspectives.

WILLING CRITICS. As you develop ideas, find one or more reliable readers who will make suggestions and criticisms when you are ready to show drafts to readers.

WRITING INSTRUCTORS. You can send e-mail to teachers and editors to ask for help with writing. You cannot count on immediate responses, but you may be able to participate in electronic conferences and consultations with instructors more immediately than in face-to-face meetings and telephone conversations.

Some instructors establish e-mail address lists for classes; they may write to a class or to individual students and receive questions, papers, and personal information from them.

19b–2 Guidelines for asking questions

Place questions first: E-mail can help you discover ideas by freewriting and brainstorming (see 3a–3, "Gather ideas"). But if you use these fluid, non-stop methods to explore your thinking as you write a message, place specific questions at the beginning of the message.

Focus your questions both on a purpose *for* writing and a purpose *in* it. For example, writing may be *for* an assignment in school or at work, a job application, or an announcement to a group. Questions about a writing situation help you clarify what your writing needs to say to specific readers. For help with matters *in* a text, you might ask about your approach to a topic, the arrangement of your points and evidence, and important details such as word choices and formatting.

Be specific: Writers always get the most useful help by asking specific questions. "What should I write?" is likely to get vague results. Instead, "I'm thinking about how music and soccer might come together in this essay" clarifies how you want your correspondent to help you.

Be flexible: A correspondent may disagree with your ideas and have experiences that enlarge your perspective, so e-mail discussions can help you develop your writing by producing ideas that you need to include as you think and write. Disagreements can be useful.

Focus on specific parts of a draft: Identify the specific sections in a draft about which you have questions or doubts. Place brackets or lines of space around these sections so your reader can find them easily.

Save questions and answers: Keep a record of your questions to help you get started again later and to remind you of writing habits you need to consider as you edit.

Check for availability: Always check the availability of anyone you want to question. Ask when particular questions may be answered before you take time out to write them, but do not impose on the time of a helper.

Manage attachments: Check whether your recipient can open and translate attached messages into readable files (see 18a–2, "E-mail header information"). If not, copy the sections relevant to your questions or the entire text into your message.

Make appointments to "talk" online: You can make appointments to talk about your work with a teacher or supervisor who has access to real-time conversation programs (see 18e, "Real-Time Conversation on the Internet"). Remember that this person probably has many other correspondents who may need help. If you initiate an exchange, expect the person you contact to determine its duration and content.

19c Tone in Questions and Answers

E-mail formats require careful attention to tone in all messages, so control the content of questions and answers to ensure their positive tone. An e-mail message with "HELP!" as a subject heading but no specific questions will produce little useful response. In addition, you cannot know your reader's mood when e-mail questions arrive. If you do not ask detailed questions, a hurried reader may assume you want only praise, not ideas for improving your writing.

→ *SECRETS OF SUCCESSFUL WRITERS* ←
Controlling Tone and Style

- To control the tone of e-mail messages, use capital letters for emphasis, if needed. But use them infrequently because THEY MAY BE READ AS SHOUTING. If you think a statement may be misunderstood, insert an explanatory comment after it in brackets or parentheses.
- To indicate titles, use quotation marks around them as you normally would in other formats, and asterisks (*) or the underscore (_) before and after words that require italics or underlining (see 5d, "Emphasizing Text"). For example, "_Hamlet_ is my favorite play."
- Do not use special characters to stimulate "smileys" and other facial expressions. Good writers use language to indicate their attitude toward a correspondent. To be sure your intended tone has been understood, read responses to your messages carefully. If you do not receive a response, ask your correspondent how your message was received.

19c–1 The tone of answers

Responding to specific e-mail questions can benefit you as directly as it does the writer asking for help. Observing another writer at work shows how documents evolve through revision and suggests new ways to choose the content of your own writing.

When you answer questions, remember that writers at work do not benefit from indifferent praise, like "Good job!" as an answer to a detailed question. Clichés and completely positive responses suggest that you have not carefully considered a writer's questions. Nor do writers trust harsh judgmental responses like "Everyone knows how to spell 'tree.'"

You may regret harsh comments. If you do not have time to answer a writer's e-mail questions thoughtfully, say that you are too busy or make it clear that you can make only a few quick comments. Do not write hasty remarks that may be taken as disrespect for the writer or as forgetfulness of the time it takes to write well.

19c–2 Guidelines for answering questions

The following guidelines will save time and make your answers more helpful.

1. In the subject line of your message, identify the question to which you are responding, especially if you have received more than one question about a document.

2. Give reasons for your answers. "I just don't like it" is not very helpful. You need not know technical terms about writing to say that you find certain words inappropriate or that you find the logic and evidence in a document unpersuasive. Explain why you do.

19d

→ *SECRETS OF SUCCESSFUL WRITERS* ←
Attachments

- Always check with anyone who says, "I'll send it to you on e-mail" to be sure your correspondent is not planning to send you an attached file you will not be able to decode. Never send an attachment unless you are sure your correspondent will be able to decode it.

---

3. When you are in doubt or do not have time to think carefully about a problem in a draft or to come up with an alternative suggestion, say so. It is more helpful to respond in this way than to leave a writer wondering about why you have not answered.

4. Include the message sent to you in your reply. You can insert comments after questions, and in drafts themselves.

5. Suggest alternatives for revising content, refining appeals to readers, and organizing a draft in general comments that you add to answers to specific questions (see 2b–1, "Answer questions").

6. Comment on the strengths of a draft, as well as its weaknesses. Identify the most intriguing ideas and most effective passages to encourage their development.

19d Controlling E-mail Style

E-mail is a form of personal communication that usually lessens the pressure to produce formal, highly formatted texts. It is often written quickly, without careful composition or word choice, so it resembles the language of telephone conversations. It is also brief, to the point, and easily read on one or two screens.

E-mail programs do not vary the font size and do not use formatting or special marks for emphasis. They allow indentations, quotation marks, and exclamation points, but not underline or italics. These formatting limitations lead some readers to view e-mail messages as more demanding, offensive, or blunt than they were intended to be.

The Next Time You Write

1. When preparing for your next writing project, use e-mail to send messages to yourself containing brainstorming, questions, and ideas.

2. Who are the reliable readers you could send your writing to? Find their e-mail addresses and add them to your e-mail address book.

3. Offer to help other writers by reading their drafts.

⟶ **20** ⟵

Electronic Writing Groups

20a E-mail Writing Groups

20b Real-time Writing Groups

The Next Time You Write

This chapter describes two possibilities for many writers using computers to complete writing projects together. It describes a model for organizing and conducting an e-mail writing group that can also be applied in other collaborative efforts. It describes how to use real-time communication software in collaborations. This chapter tells how to organize and assign tasks in an e-mail group and addresses making general and specific comments. It explains real-time writing situations and gives advice about effective synchronous writing with others and about moving from these online conversations to formal documents.

20a E-mail Writing Groups

E-mail can help groups of students and co-workers interpret information and complete group writing projects. A group can share responses to documents and together decide topics, refine ideas, collaborate on information gathering and composing, interpret assignments, and accomplish practical work. A group can connect with local or distant groups to share information and ideas.

20a–1 Organizing e-mail writing groups

To organize an e-mail writing group, first gather e-mail addresses for each group member. With this list, the administrator of your e-mail system can establish a mailing list on your network or each member of the group can create a "distribution list" address in his or her address book. This e-mail address will distribute messages to everyone on the list (see 18b, "Mailing Lists").

20a–2 Assigning tasks

Groups working on a collaborative project may assign functions to individual members who agree to the following roles.

Group manager: This member keeps the writing project on schedule by defining deadlines, scheduling times for online conferences or in-person meetings, and communicating the status of the project with other members of the group.

Word processing manager: This member helps with technical matters like the compatibility of word processing formats and oversees the formatting of the final document.

Wordsmith: This person is responsible for editing and reediting the writing using reliable writing guides.

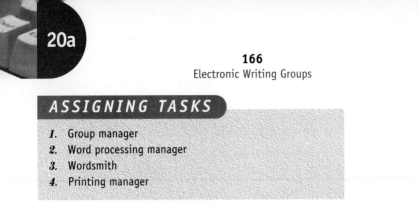

ASSIGNING TASKS

1. Group manager
2. Word processing manager
3. Wordsmith
4. Printing manager

Printing manager: This member prints and delivers the completed document.

If a group is not large enough to assign all of these tasks individually, members can use this list as a guide to coordinate efforts. If there are more than enough members, the group can distribute research, drafting, and editing tasks among them.

20a–3 Making general comments

Members of the group must use common language to communicate clearly to everyone. The following suggestions identify terms for discussing texts you write as a group.

PURPOSE. Purpose is the first consideration in any discussion of a text. A group needs to understand both a purpose *for* writing (to fulfill an assignment? to report to another group? to petition an organization?) and a purpose *in* writing (to interpret another document according to a particular frame of reference? to evaluate a performance or policy in terms of practical successes? to analyze an action, event, or scientific phenomenon?). A text may present a discovery of new information, verify that its writers understand information presented to them, explore and analyze the implications of information, or demonstrate expertise of another kind. Considerations of purpose determine what a document says and does for its writers and its readers.

After a group agrees, at least provisionally, about the purpose of a specific reading or writing task, all members can refer to it as they work. Decisions about the meaning of particular parts of readings, the way to introduce a jointly written or individual text, and how to format for printing all depend on identifying purposes for and in a text. A purpose guides what to say and determines information and reasoning that should be emphasized.

READERS. It is important to clarify the identity of actual readers of a text, whether they are the group that a reading or report was sent to or those who will read the group's writing. Every text has not only actual readers but a wider range of "ideal" or "implied" readers—identities brought to mind by the writing itself. An advertisement for an expensive car, for instance, invokes an ideal audience of people who can afford the car and who want the status usually associated with it, even when many actual readers of the ad cannot afford and do not want to buy it.

Actual readers: Choices about examples, language, and the appearance of a text all depend on the expectations of actual readers. Effective writing makes statements its readers will respect, even if they may disagree with them. Writers must consider the evidence they need to support their statements and the reasoning they apply to the evidence in terms of the knowledge and values their readers share.

Implied readers: Friends, an instructor, or other identifiable audiences may be actual readers of a document. But its idealized readers may be a general public, professionals in the field of interest addressed by the topic, an imagined group of voters and other decision makers, and so on. Some writing idealizes women or men as readers, although both will actually read it.

When group members comment on its reading- or writing-in-progress, they should address how well a text considers its actual readers while invoking idealized responses. Check how elements that attract attention—a title or formatting, for instance—appeal to actual readers. In addition, how well do its points and examples appeal to the ideal reader who would understand and respond to them?

EVIDENCE. Depending on its purpose and readers, a text may make all its points with examples that suggest generalized points, as fiction and poetry do. It also may include references to other sources in the form of quick comments or use extended, referenced quotations and paraphrases from experts and authorities. Depending on its intended audience, it may reason about and draw inferences from commonly known information, as editorials often do. It may demonstrate its points scientifically, on the basis of data, statistics, and experimental results. Examples, references to sources, reasoning, and experimental data are all specific kinds of evidence.

Groups need to consider the nature and scope of the evidence used to support the points under consideration. Is this evidence sufficiently familiar to support the points made, but not too obvious? Does the document reveal enough about the content of its sources to stimulate agreement with its points? Are the facts presented currently accepted? Are the inferences drawn from them logical? Are actual and possible objections addressed with evidence from reliable sources? A group should answer these questions thoroughly.

20a–4 Making specific comments on style

Readers often interpret the meaning of what they read by noticing how its style supports, or in some cases weakens, its purpose for specific audiences. Group comments may separately address sentence patterns, word choices, and formatting. Group members might focus on each of these issues in turn to suggest needed changes.

To check the style and formatting of a document you write, review handbooks, especially their guidelines for revision (see 3c, "Revising"). Find models of documents written for similar purposes and audiences and compare their formats to your visual choices.

The language of effective writing depends on conventions in the community that it addresses. Highly specialized or overly general word choices can undermine your purpose, so be guided by the terms and references that similar documents commonly use.

20a–5 Remaining flexible

Obviously, not all language is appropriate for all readers; only certain kinds of evidence will accomplish certain purposes; and some presentations are more formal than others. Consider these variables as a group to analyze and write documents. Think of them as interdependent choices that must be negotiated among the group's members.

20a–6 Acknowledging e-mail help

When you write with a group, list in alphabetical order all of its members as authors of a document.

When you receive e-mail help with writing of any kind, include an acknowledgment of the help and its source. Cite a news group or mailing list as you would a letter, using a format appropriate to your document. For example, to acknowledge help with writing this chapter, we would use the following note:

Hollowell, John. "E-mail groups." E-mail to the authors. 8 August 1995.

Remember to let those who helped you know that you are citing them and thank them.

20b Real-time Writing Groups

Some local networks allow groups to hold online conferences on the Internet (see 18e, "Real-time Conversation on the Internet") or on their own network. Instead of waiting for e-mail, group members schedule times to meet and simultaneously hold textual, real-time synchronous electronic conversations.

20b–1 Effective real-time writing

To be an effective contributor in a synchronous conversation, you need to develop ways to draw attention to your points and questions while responding to what others say. You can keep an exchange going by adding ideas, elaborating on what others say, reconsidering your statements, and acknowledging how others influence your thoughts.

Making concise points in organized, easily readable language is an involved process, even if you have time to edit and recheck drafts. But in instantaneous written exchanges, it is difficult to control all the aspects of effective contributions with confidence, even when you write anonymously.

Some writers understandably respond to these pressures in ways that weaken the cooperative spirit of any successful conversation. Participants may attempt to dominate a conversation by raising side issues or by evaluating what others say on personal grounds rather than on grounds related to the topic. They may demand attention by writing overly long responses that require too much time for reading and also prevent them from having time to read others' statements carefully.

Fears of writing poorly, of meeting opposition, of making misstatements, and of not receiving responses can also result in a writer's withdrawing from an exchange. Some writers become silent and write only brief comments that repeat and agree with what others have said but do not develop the topic. But every participant shares responsibility for the success of real-time conversations. They are relatively low-risk settings in which to practice writing.

20b–2 Using real-time conversations to develop ideas

It is obvious that discussions of topics for writing by a well-informed group help prepare for writing. But to ensure that conversations are helpful, you need specific ways to connect them to writing after they end. You can copy a transcript of a conversation or make notes about it in a file you will use later. Answers to the following questions can help you transform this record into a source for your writing.

RELEVANT STATEMENTS.   What parts of the conversation obviously were related to the point you want to make? There may be only a few exchanges that were directly related to your approach, but mark any you may want to consider as you write. Copy or summarize them in notes for your draft.

RETHINKING YOUR APPROACH.   Did you reconsider your approach during the conversation? If so, in what way? If not, were you too reserved about stating your intentions and asking for responses? Write a statement about how the conversation changed or reinforced your attitude or choice of content.

NEW POINTS TO INCLUDE.   If you changed your mind significantly during conversation, what new points will you make? What points did others make that you need to acknowledge? Make notes of them. Include any new information you may need to gather to support your new conclusions.

OPPOSING VIEWS. What opposition was there to the main point you plan to make in your writing, either directly or in discussion of related issues? Was any of your evidence questioned on the basis of fact or the reliability of its source? What was the specific nature of this opposition? List these objections and possible responses to them. What additional information will you need to account for opposing points of view and to acknowledge other perspectives? How did your thinking change in response to questions and criticism?

20b–3 How to improve real-time writing

As with any specialized writing, synchronous writing requires and rewards practice. You can work on improving the separate skills needed to participate fully. Here are some guidelines for managing your writing in this situation.

Identify any basics you need to practice: If you type and read slowly, practice copying brief dialogues and quickly reading texts. Rapidly identify the main point of a passage, the issues it raises, and possible responses to it. Write responses and questions about reading as quickly as you can, and reread your writing. How would you answer your own questions? Why?

Identify your usual conversational style: When you talk face to face in groups, do you listen carefully to others or interrupt before they finish? Do you lead or follow? Do you enjoy making bold statements that get attention or do you tend to stay on the sidelines? Do you start side conversations to become comfortable within a larger group? List these and any other habits you use in conversations. How might they affect your contributions in written conversations? Practice writing dialogue that demonstrates interactions you value.

Prepare for a synchronous conversation: Read materials relevant to the topic or problem that will be discussed, and note responses and questions. If you do not know what will be discussed, review earlier conversations and relevant materials to connect the statements of specific participants to points in the discussion. How did comments that received attention address the topic and respond to other participants? How did they extend or

HOW TO IMPROVE REAL-TIME WRITING

1. Identify any basics you need to practice.
2. Identify your usual conversational style.
3. Prepare for a synchronous conversation.
4. Identify your goals in advance.
5. Analyze success in transcripts.
6. Analyze missteps.

limit lines of conversation? If you do not prepare, enter a new conversation with an open and curious attitude, not defensively.

Identify your goals in advance: What do you want to take from a particular synchronous conversation? Choose one or two skills you would like to address as you participate. Do you want to contribute more frequently, receive more responses, or work toward some other goal? Will the discussion help with a specific assignment or problem later?

Analyze success in transcripts: Print a transcript at the close of a conversation. A printer may be attached to the networked computers; if not, save the conversation as a file to print elsewhere. If it is impossible to print, find a transcript of an earlier exchange in which you were not a participant.

Work with a partner or in a group to identify examples of the following qualities of successful contributions.

1. They develop ideas about the topic by bringing up new points and adding information that supports them.

2. They receive positive or opposing responses soon after they appear.

3. They disagree with other statements by focusing on their logic and development or errors of fact, not by using general language or criticizing the writer.

4. They do not abruptly change the subject, stereotype the group, or invoke "common sense" and what "everyone knows" to silence a disagreement.

5. They are sometimes humorous, but not sarcastic or difficult to understand.

Analyze missteps: Reread the transcript to find examples of unsuccessful contributions. How might they be restated to contribute more to the exchange? Rewrite a few of them to make them read like successful contributions.

20b–4 From conversation to formal document

Synchronous conversations allow writers to test, develop, refine, and revise ideas about specific topics. They also show that your ideas need to be stated in relation to readers' possible responses to them. To use a transcript and notes about it as you write, copy relevant portions of the transcript with your own comments during and after the conversation into a notes file for your writing. In that file, try out one or more of the following ways of using the notes.

Write dialogue: Create a dialogue in your document, alternating questions about your approach and possible answers to them. In addition, write alternating pairs of statements showing opposing and qualifying comments by others on your statements. Which of these pairs do you need to address in your document? After each pair of questions and answers, or a significant statement and opposition to it, write a brief paragraph to state a new combination of these ideas.

Identify stimulating points: Identify comments that received the most responses in the conversation. Write sentences that imitate their ways of drawing attention to new perspectives. How do they introduce a comment? Do they acknowledge the statements of other participants? Notice how they respect what others say but make their own positions clear and offer specific evidence to support them.

Choose points to pursue: Identify exchanges that you find especially provocative. Write questions they raise for you now and possible ways to develop answers to them in your writing.

Write an introduction: Write a summary of the synchronous conversation as a draft introductory paragraph for your writing. For instance, begin with "Some people think that . . . ," and summarize the most frequently emphasized point made in the discussion.

Follow this summary with "But others believe . . ." (or "have evidence to show" or "disagree because"), again using opinions stated among the group.

After this summary, state your main point in a sentence that reveals the approach you plan to take. This statement should close your introduction.

Use the conversation as a source: Make a list of relevant examples and sources mentioned in the transcript. Find references to material you want to include, so that you can cite them as you draft and revise your writing.

Acknowledge the conversation: After you complete a draft, reread it to note places where the participants in the conversation would agree or disagree with your points or want to qualify them. Decide if you need to acknowledge these perspectives in your revised draft. Make notes about how to do so by referring to ideas, specific people, or the sources for these ideas.

Manage these responses to synchronous conversations as you do any notes for writing, choosing those that help you develop what you want to say for a particular purpose in the most effective way (see 7e, "Research Logs and Storage").

The Next Time You Write

1. The next time you read someone's writing, use the questions about purpose, readers, and evidence (see 20a–3, "Making general comments") as a basis to give feedback on their writing.

2. Review chapter 19, "Using E-mail to Improve Your Writing," and 18a, "Electronic Mail (e-mail)."

3. Review 18e, "Real-Time Conversation on the Internet."

21

Writing for the World Wide Web

This chapter describes how you can use the World Wide Web to distribute your writing. It introduces Web pages and hypertexts; talks about reasons for writing Web pages; outlines the basics of HyperText Markup Language (HTML) which must be used to create Web pages; and tells how to write, publish, and advertise Web pages—including tips for effective Web page design.

21a Web Pages, Home Pages, and Hypertexts

E-mail, news group postings, and texts available from FTP and Gopher sites all constitute simple forms of electronic publishing. But when you receive these electronic publications, they are usually presented as text-only documents, without the added emphasis and graphics available in printed publications. The World Wide Web (WWW or Web), however, makes it possible to publish electronic texts with formatting: varying fonts and font sizes, using bold, italicized, and underlined text, aligning text, and importing graphics. The World Wide Web can also link text and graphics to other Web pages and Internet sites.

You connect to the World Wide Web with software called a Web browser. Programs like Netscape, Mosaic, Lynx, and others connect you to several types of Internet addresses (URLs; see 17b-4, "Combining tasks"). World Wide Web addresses begin with "http://." For example, Prentice Hall's home page address is http://www.prenhall.com/. Web addresses may be cited without surrounding punctuation, or inside "less than" (<) and "greater than" (>) signs, or inside quotation marks.

When you open a Web browser and connect to a Web address, you will see a visual representation of a page. Web pages can contain text and graphics that are linked to other parts of the same Web page, to other Web pages, or to other Internet resources such as FTP sites and news groups. Text or graphics that are coded to allow you to jump to other places are called "hypertext." Hypertext may allow you to jump from a word to an image, or the reverse, or from a word to related images or phrases. You activate the link simply by clicking the mouse on the text or graphics that are highlighted or underlined.

If you are using a graphical Web browser (such as Netscape Navigator for Macintosh or Windows), you can see a Web page by opening a connection to its address (see 17b–4, "Combining tasks"). You use your mouse to select links and move around the Web site.

Figure 21.1 Web Site Accessed with a Graphical Web Browser

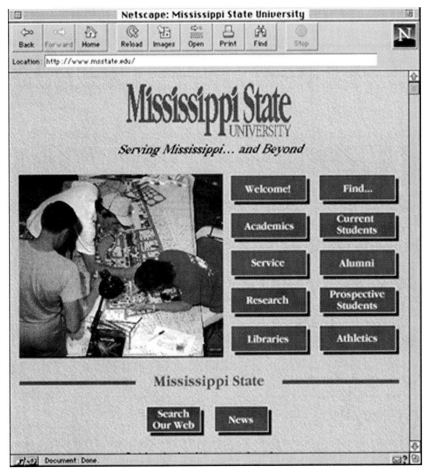

If you are using a nongraphical Web browser (such as Lynx), you use the tab key or arrow keys and press Enter to select links.

A home page (sometimes called a welcome page) is the first page of a Web site. This page links readers to other pages at the Web site. Organizations and individuals use home pages to distribute information about themselves. Many companies now include their home page address on employee business cards, stationery, and advertisements. Home pages might display contact information like phone and fax numbers, addresses, and office hours.

Figure 21.2 Web Site Accessed with a Text-based Web Browser

```
                                        Mississippi State University


    Mississippi State University
    Serving Mississippi... and Beyond
    The Picture of the Day Welcome! | Find... | Academics | Students |
    Service | Alumni | Research | Prospective Stud ents | Libraries |
    Athletics |
    ---------Mississippi State University ----------
    Search Our Web | News |
    For information about this page, contact Bennet George.
    For information about this server, contact webmaster@msstate.edu.
    For information about Mississippi State University, contact
    msuinfo@ur.msstate.edu.
    Last modified: Tuesday, 30-Apr-96 15:34:13 CDT.
    URL: http://www.msstate.edu/index.html
    Mississippi State University is an equal opportunity institution.








Commands: Use arrow keys to move, '?' for help, 'q' to quit, '<-' to go back.
  Arrow keys: Up and Down to move. Right to follow a link; Left to go back.
  H)elp O)ptions P)rint G)o M)ain screen Q)uit /=search [delete]=history list   █
```

21b Why Write Web Pages?

You do not have to write Web pages to explore the World Wide Web. But there are many benefits of writing your own Web pages.

21b–1 To make a starting point

Web browser software allows you to set up "bookmarks" that list Internet addresses and Web sites you access often or want to return to in the future. If you share a computer with other people, however, bookmarks may have been erased when you return. Making your own Web page with a list of Internet addresses to which you frequently return allows you to access this information easily. This Web page can be your starting point for exploring the Internet.

21b–2 To catalog and link research sources

You can link related Web pages, electronic journal addresses and entire articles, FTP sites that contain important files, and other sources into one Web page. This Web page can be updated frequently while you work on a research project. Once you complete a project, you can make this page available on the Web so that others can find these related sources.

21b–3 To help others reach you

When you write e-mail messages or post messages to news groups, you can include your home page address in your signature. For example, if your name is John Clarke, you might use the following signature at the end of an e-mail message: "John Clarke http://www.clarke.com/~john/." (See 18a-3, "Helpful hints.")

If you are unsure whether your correspondents have access to the World Wide Web, use a longer signature that includes contact information plus your home page address.

21b–4 To share information about you and publish your writing

You can include links from your home page to other Web pages that display your résumé, an autobiography, pictures, or starting point Web pages that you use. This information will be immediately available to employers and schools to which you apply and to other correspondents. You can also set up links from your home page to pages that contain your writing. Instead of sending your paper to a friend using e-mail, for example, you can send a short e-mail message telling your friend the Web address of your paper. Most Web browsers will allow your readers to write e-mail messages to you about a Web page. They can include in the response the document itself, with comments.

21b–5 To manage group projects

Web pages are useful for members of a group working together on short projects. They can display schedules, questions, and members' work. They can distribute updated documents and other current information a group needs. A class Web page, for example, might display a current copy of a class syllabus, lecture notes, and requirements for upcoming assignments. The interactive capabilities of Web browsers such as sending e-mail or accessing news groups make it possible for group members to use these resources while working on the project.

21b–6 To learn more about writing

Web pages are excellent ways to experiment with different forms of writing, including interactive forms of electronic publishing to unknown audiences. To write for the Web you must understand a unique feature of electronic communication. Electronic hypertexts are marked links that are highlighted in color or underlined or both.

To create a hypertext, you encode a piece of text (usually a word or phrase) that is related to another Web site or another location in your Web site. Readers of Web pages can follow a path from one to another link. The links may connect related electronic sources or, within a document, locate all references to a word or image; they allow readers to move freely among the concepts in and connected to your writing.

This process uniquely demonstrates the relationship between content and structure in a text. Making appropriate hypertext links among words, phrases, and pictures can help you check your writing for coherence. (Even without an actual Web page, linking ideas by marking words that carry a theme through a text will show you how readers can, or cannot, easily follow ideas in your writing.)

21c HyperText Markup Language (HTML)

When you open a Web page, you see a representation of a file (called the "source file") that the writer of the page constructed. Source files contain the text the writer wants to display on a Web page plus coded instructions that tell a Web browser how to format the text, how to show graphics, how to create hypertext links, and how to arrange everything the reader sees.

To accomplish this combination of writing, formatting, and linking, the writer of a Web page must use HyperText Markup Language (HTML). HTML is a code made up of letters and symbols that Web browsers interpret. Combinations of these symbols, called "tags," in source files specify the design of Web pages. For example, <b> is the HTML tag that instructs the Web browser to display the text following it in boldface.

Figures 21.3 and 21.4 show, respectively, an HTML source file and what a reader sees when a Web browser displays the file.

There are several HTML tags, and many being developed. Table 21.1 indicates a few of the frequently used HTML tags.

21d How to Write and Publish Web Pages

Writing effective corporate and institutional Web pages takes practice and some expertise in design and publishing. But any writer can learn the basics required to write an HTML file to create an effective personal or group Web page. If you know HTML code, you can work with word processing software or a simple text editor (such as BBEdit) and a Web browser. Even if you do not know HTML code, you can use programs with built-in buttons and functions that make it easy to create Web pages. At http://www.shareware.com/ you can search for HTML editors to use on your particular computer. Your word processing program or Web browser may also have built-in HTML editing features.

Writing for the World Wide Web involves exploration and experimentation. With the View Source command in your Web browser, for instance,

Figure 21.3 HTML Source File Viewed by a Text Editor

```
<HTML>
<HEAD>
<TITLE>Clayton's Home Page</TITLE>
<!--Started this page November 9, 1996.<--i>
</HEAD>

<BODY>
<CENTER>
<B>"I'm writing for the World Wide Web!" --</B>
<I>Clayton Bowers</I>
<H1>Welcome to Clayton's Home Page</H1>
</CENTER>

Thanks for visiting my Web page.<BR>

I started writing for the World Wide Web a few weeks ago.<P>

<HR>
<P>

<H3>Interesting Links</H3>
<UL>
<LI><A HREF="http://www.yahoo.com/">Yahoo</A>, a popular place to begin surfing the Internet.
<LI>Purdue University's <A HREF="http://owl.english.purdue.edu/">Online Writing Lab</A>
<LI>The Complete Works of <A HREF="http://the-tech.mit.edu/Shakespeare/works.html">Shakespeare</A>
comes in handy when looking for quotes.
<LI>My <A HREF="resume.html">resume</A> is now available.
</UL>
<P>

<IMG SRC="clayton.gif">
<P>

<HR>
<CENTER>
Send me e-mail at <A HREF="mailto:clayton@fsu.edu">clayton.bowers@fsu.edu</A>
<CENTER>

</BODY>
</HTML>
```

you can see how others use HTML codes in their Web pages and you can imitate them.

When you begin writing for the World Wide Web, you will benefit from specialized help. Experienced friends and co-workers can help you quickly correct simple mistakes and teach you to use HTML. You can also find many HTML and World Wide Web guides on the Internet. To find online manuals and tutorials, search at http://www.yahoo.com/ for "World Wide Web" and "HTML." Many helpful books are available. (See "Additional Sources" on page 185.)

BRAINSTORM. Take time to brainstorm your purpose for writing a Web page. To get ideas for your Web page, list possible content and links to other pages. Then edit your list to focus your page on a particular effect you want. Keep in mind that any personal information you include will be available to anyone with a Web browser.

GATHER CONTENT. You may gather content for your Web page from many sources. For example, you can include entire texts, notes of interesting Internet sites, and photographs and graphics you make or copy from public sources. Always cite the source of materials you copy. Check

Figure 21.4 HTML Source File Viewed by a Web Browser

whether you need permission to use any types of files you want to put on your pages. If you want to use materials not already in computer files, you can type or scan texts and scan and reduce the file size of pictures. Place all of these files in one folder or directory.

You will need to use specialized software to reduce the file size of graphics and other multimedia files because you may not have enough disk space

TABLE 21.1 BASIC HTML CODES

HTML TAGS (type them precisely)	Name	What do they do?
<HTML>[text]</HTML>*	HTML	Conventional tags used to indicate that the file is an HTML source file
<HEAD>[text]</HEAD>	Header	Usually the title and comments are placed in the header.
<TITLE>[text]</TITLE>	Title	Title displayed at the top of the Web page
<!--[text]-->	Comment	Does not display when file is viewed by a Web browser Usually used by Web writers to write notes to themselves
<BODY>[text]</BODY>	Body	The majority of your Web page goes here.
<CENTER>[text]</CENTER>	Center	Centers text
<B>[text]</B>	Boldface	Makes text boldface
<I>[text]</I>	Italics	Italicizes text
<H1>[text]</H1>	First-level heading	Enlarges texts and sets it off from other text
 	Line break	Equivalent of "Return"
<P>	Paragraph	Equivalent of two "Returns" or two line breaks
<HR>	Horizontal rule	Line break, a visual line, and another line break
<H3>[text]</H3>	Third-level heading	Enlarges text and sets it off from other text
<UL>[text]</UL>	Unordered list	Starts a list
<LI>	List	When used with the <UL> tag, bullets each item

*Paired codes like this one are used to indicate the beginning and end of certain elements or instructions.

(continued)

TABLE 21.1 CONTINUED

HTML TAGS (type them precisely)	Name	What do they do?
<A HREF="[Internet address]**">**[text to be linked]**</A>**	Link to Internet address	Creates a link to an Internet URL. Can use various protocols such as gopher://,ftp://, and http://
<A HREF="[file name]**">** [text to be linked]**</A>**	Link to a file	Used to connect Web pages at a single site
<A HREF="mailto: [e-mail address]**">** [text to be linked]**</A>**	Send e-mail	Opens an e-mail compose window in most browsers
<IMG SRC="[graphic file name]**">**	Displays a graphic	Will display graphics files
<PRE>[text]**</PRE>**	Preformatted text	Displays text using the text's tabs and returns

to store large files. In addition, it takes much longer for Web browsers to display large graphics files. If you are new to using graphics, you may want to postpone learning how to include them until you get help from an experienced writer of Web pages. You can then practice including graphics and test the results and their efficiency in relation to your purposes.

SKETCH THE PAGE DESIGN. As you explore Web sites, notice how they are designed and organized in ways you may want to use in your own page. Sketch out preliminary ideas about how you want your Web page to look. Outline the content of your Web page and links, imagining how it can fit your purpose.

CREATE YOUR HTML SOURCE FILE. Open your word processor or your text or HTML editor. Save a document as "source.html" (or "source.htm" if using DOS or any version of Windows lower than Windows 95). It is conventional to name home page files "index.html" (or "index.htm"). Other Web pages have various file names, but most end with ".html" (or ".htm") so they are easily recognizable. If you are using word processing software to write your pages, save these HTML files as "text only."

It's conventional to begin your HTML source files by typing "<html>." Next, type "<head>" and "<title>." Then type the title of your Web page. After the title type "</title>" and "</head>." (HTML tags are typed inside "less than" (<) and "greater than" (>) signs.

After this introductory material, type "<body>." Insert the text of the content you want to place on your page. After the text is in the source file, you must code it with HTML tags (see Table 21.1). There is usually a tag at the beginning and at the end of content to be formatted, but some tags, like the paragraph tag (<p>) and the line break tag (<br>) stand alone. For example, the "start bold" tag is <b> and the "stop bold" tag is </b>. If you were writing a Web page and you wanted the word *cannot* in the sentence "I cannot find it" to be in boldface, in your HTML file you would type "I <b>cannot</b> find it."

Save often. Spell-check and proofread your writing. End your source file by typing "</body> </html>".

VIEW YOUR HTML FILE USING YOUR WEB BROWSER.   To see how your HTML source file will be viewed by a Web browser, launch your Web browser and use the Open File command to open "source.html" (or the name of your source file). If your computer cannot simultaneously open both your Web browser and the program you are using to write the source file, quit the program you are using to write your source file, launch your Web browser, and use the Open File command to open your source file.

EDIT YOUR HTML SOURCE FILE.   You will probably need to edit your source file to improve its appearance and ensure that hypertext links you have inserted actually work and are useful to your readers. When you see problems in the Web browser display of your HTML file, go back to your word processor or HTML editor to find typos and errors in your HTML codes. Here are some common problems:

1. Did you save the file as "text only"?

2. Did you omit needed ending HTML tags (such as </b>)?

3. Did you overlook typos in the Internet addresses or in the file names used as links?

Be sure to save your changes. Then review your Web page again for any additional changes. Repeat this process if necessary.

PUBLISH YOUR WEB PAGES.   To make Web pages available to everyone on the Internet, you must copy them to a World Wide Web server. If you have an e-mail account and Internet access, ask your system administrator if you also have access to a Web server. If so, your system administrator may have documents that explain how to copy your source file to the Web server. If this service is not available, try an Internet access provider or commercial online service (see 16a-3, "Internet access").

After you have access to a Web server, follow instructions for naming and saving your source and graphics files, if any, and transferring them to the appropriate directory. When your files have been copied to a Web server, open a Web browser and connect to the "http://" address of your Web pages. If you have trouble connecting, check with your system administrator to be sure that you followed your system's procedures correctly.

ADVERTISE YOUR WEB PAGES. When your Web page is accessible, you can advertise its availability to various Web sites on the Internet. List and describe your Web page at a Web site called "Submit It!" at http://www. submit-it.com/ by completing the electronic form at this site. This process will link your Web page to the largest cataloging and indexing sites on the Web.

If you are an active participant in a news group, a discussion list, or other groups, you may want to announce your Web page to them. You can also include your Web address in your e-mail signature (see 18a–3, "Helpful hints").

21e Tips for Effective Web Page Design

Writing and coding Web pages may tempt you to focus on formatting, not content. These guidelines, however, will help you focus on content first.

1. Determine how long it takes a Web browser to display your Web pages. Make needed changes in your text to reduce excessive loading time.

2. Focus the information you display on each Web page. Keep your pages informative but efficiently designed.

3. Verify that all links on your Web pages are working correctly and that they have been explained. Hypertext links should index your content, connect to relevant information, and be easily followed. Avoid sending your readers to other Internet sites unless there is a clear purpose for doing so.

4. Avoid large background files, graphics files, or multimedia files. The time needed to display them may irritate Web page readers.

The Next Time You Write

1. Explore the World Wide Web to find and note the addresses of places that have well-organized, easily followed Web pages. Refer to them as you write your own pages. Imitate those that fit your purposes.

2. View HTML source files of one or two Web pages to determine the functions the HTML codes perform.

3. Use the codes defined in this chapter to write a brief Web page. Save it as a text-only file and then open it with a Web browser to see the results.

4. Follow the instructions in this chapter to design home pages for more than one purpose. For instance, you might design one page with your family members in mind and another for business purposes.

Additional Sources

Style Books

Hickey, Dona J. *Developing a Written Voice*. Mountain View, CA: Mayfield, 1993. Although this is a book about style, it is not categorized according to stylistic features. Instead, it discusses style in terms of appropriate voice for a given writing situation.

Lanham, Richard A. *Revising Prose*. 2nd ed. New York: Macmillan, 1987. This compact book discusses appropriate academic style with an emphasis on revision and editing.

————. *Revising Business Prose*. 2nd ed. New York: Macmillan, 1987. Emphasizes a verbal style business prose and offers numerous examples from a variety of business formats.

Roman, Kenneth. *Writing That Works*. 2nd ed. New York: HarperPerennial, 1992. Stresses the purpose and audience for business writing situations as well as the need to make points quickly.

Williams, Joseph. *Style: Ten Lessons in Clarity and Grace*. 4th ed. New York: HarperCollins, 1994. Provides a model of an academic style appropriate for general use and offers detailed explanations of its principles with copious examples and exercises.

————. *Style: Toward Clarity and Grace*. Chicago: U of Chicago P, 1990. Omits exercises in favor of more comprehensive, detailed explanations and examples. Provides advice concerning appropriate academic style and writing clearly about complex subjects.

Handbooks

Corbett, Edward P. J. *The Little English Handbook*. 6th ed. New York: HarperCollins, 1992. A compact account of the format, grammar, style, mechanics, and documentation necessary for correct standard usage.

Hacker, Diana. *A Writer's Reference*. 3rd ed. Boston: Bedford Books, 1995. A detailed presentation of correct grammar, punctuation, mechanics, and documentation. Includes a special section for writers for whom English is a second language.

Hodges, John C., et al. *The Harbrace College Handbook*. 12th ed. Fort Worth: Harcourt, 1994. Provides exhaustive coverage of all facets of standard usage.

Style Manuals for Various Fields

American Institute of Physics. *AIP Style Manual*. 4th ed. New York: AIP, 1990.

American Mathematical Society. *A Manual for Authors of Mathematical Papers*. Rev. ed. Providence: AMS, 1990.

American Psychological Association. *Publication Manual of the American Psychological Association*. 4th ed. Washington: APA, 1994.

Council of Biology Editors. *Scientific Style and Format: The CBE Manual for Authors, Editors, and Publishers*. 6th ed. New York: Cambridge UP, 1994.

Dodd, Janet S., ed. *The ACS Style Guide: A Manual for Authors and Editors*. Washington: American Chemical Soc., 1986.

Gibaldi, Joseph. *MLA Handbook for Writers of Research Papers*. 4th ed. New York: Modern Language Assn. of America, 1995.

Harvard Law Review. *A Uniform System of Citation*. 15th ed. Cambridge: Harvard Law Review, 1991.

Iverson, Cheryl, et al. *American Medical Association Manual of Style*. 8th ed. Baltimore: Williams and Wilkins, 1988.

University of Chicago Press. *The Chicago Manual of Style*. 14th ed. Chicago: U of Chicago P, 1993.

Word Processing Style and Electronic Research Citations

Recent editions of style manuals include information about the documentation of online sources. The *MLA Handbook*, for example, contains a very good section on citing electronic publications, CD-ROMs, and online databases. Always make sure that you are consulting the most recent edition of any style manual. The following sources are dedicated to how to use unique features of computers to punctuate and how to cite electronic sources.

Li, Xia, and Nancy Crane. *Electronic Style: A Guide to Citing Electronic Information*. Westport: Meckler, 1993.

Williams, Robin. *The Mac Is Not a Typewriter*. Berkeley: Peachpit, 1992.

———. *The PC Is Not a Typewriter*. Berkeley: Peachpit, 1992.

The Internet and the World Wide Web

Sources about the Internet and the World Wide Web are proliferating at an astonishing rate. The following texts are valuable as we write this, but always consult the most recent edition of a text.

Barron, Billy, et al. *The Internet Unleashed 1996*. Indianapolis: Sams, 1996. Basic introduction to the Internet. Focuses on everything from the history of the Internet to using e-mail and surfing the Web.

December, John, and Neil Randall. *The World Wide Web Unleashed*. 2nd ed. Indianapolis: Sams, 1995. Basic introduction to the World Wide Web, focusing on browsing throughout its various services. Assumes Internet experience.

Kehoe, Brendan P. *Zen and the Art of the Internet*. 3rd ed. Englewood Cliffs: Prentice, 1994. Oriented toward the novice Internet user; focuses on e-mail, news groups, and Telnet databases.

Krol, Ed. *The Whole Internet User's Guide and Catalog*. 2nd ed. Sebastopol, CA: O'Reilly, 1994. Perhaps the best overall guide to the Internet, from e-mail and Gopher to the World Wide Web. Includes history and comprehensive instruction and catalog information for the Internet.

Lemay, Laura. *Teach Yourself Web Publishing with HTML in 14 Days*. Indianapolis: Sams, 1995. Details how to write and design Web pages using HTML. Covers advanced topics, including forms and adding multimedia, and discusses new HTML codes.

Figure credits

Figures 1.1, 15.1, 18.5: System 7.5 © 1983–1995 Apple Computer, Inc. Used with permission. Apple and the Apple logo are registered trademarks of Apple Computer, Inc. All Rights Reserved.

Figures 1.1, 2.2, 2.3, 2.4, 4.1: Screen shots reproduced with permission from Microsoft Corporation.

Figures 1.2, 1.3: Reproduced courtesy of Corel Corp. WordPerfect® is a registered trademark of Corel Corp.

Figures 9.1, 9.2: Reproduced courtesy of Marriott Library, University of Utah.

Figure 9.3: This screen is reproduced with permission of SilverPlatter Information, Inc. © 1986–1995 SilverPlatter International N.V.

Figure 15.1: Reproduced courtesy of Adobe Systems, Inc.

Figure 13.1: Reproduced courtesy of the Princeton Review.

Figure 16.1: Reproduced courtesy of America Online. Copyright 1996 America Online, Inc. All rights reserved.

Figure 16.2: Reproduced courtesy of XMISSION and NCSA/University of Illinois-Champaign.

Figure 17.1: Reproduced courtesy of University of Utah and NCSA/University of Illinois-Champaign.

Figure 17.2: Reproduced courtesy of University of Minnesota.

Figure 17.3, 17.6, 21.1, 21.4: Reproduced courtesy of Netscape Communications Corp. Netscape Communications Corporation has not authorized, sponsored, or endorsed, or approved this publication and is not responsible for its content. Netscape and the Netscape Communications Corporate Logos, are trademarks and trade names of Netscape Communications Corporation. All other product names and/or logos are trademarks of their respective owners.

Figure 17.4: Reproduced courtesy of Harvard University Library and NCSA/University of Illinois-Champaign.

Figures 17.5, 18.3: Reproduced courtesy of Dartmouth College Computer Center.

Figure 17.6: Reproduced courtesy of Jeremy Hylton.

Figure 18.1: Reproduced courtesy of Qualcomm, Inc.

Figure 18.3: Reproduced courtesy of Fashion Internet.

Figure 18.4: Reproduced courtesy of NCSA/University of Illinois-Champaign.

Figure 18.5: Reproduced courtesy of Blue Cow Software.

Figure 18.6 (a-c): Reproduced courtesy of Miami University and Suzanne Bonefas and NCSA/University of Illinois-Champaign.

Figures 21.1, 21.2: Reproduced courtesy of Mississippi State University.

Figure 21.2: Reproduced courtesy of the Free Software Foundation, Inc.

INDEX